Archaeological
Guide to Rome

ARCHAEOLOGICAL GUIDE TO ROME

EDITED BY
ADRIANO LA REGINA

Ministero dei Beni
e delle Attività Culturali e del Turismo

Soprintendenza Speciale per il Colosseo,
il Museo Nazionale Romano
e l'Area Archeologica di Roma

The Roman Forum

The Palatine
and the Circus Maximus

The Capitol
and The Capitoline
Museums

The Imperial Forums

The Coliseum

The Domus Aurea

Electa

On the cover
The Colosseum and the Arch
of Constantine from the Temple
of Venus and Roma
(photo by Bruno Angeli)

Back cover
The Roman Forum
(photo by Bruno Angeli)

Opposite title page
House of Augustus, detail
of the decoration of the Room
of the Pine Festoons

On page 6
Statue of Hercules. Rome,
Capitoline Museums, Exedra
of Marcus Aurelius

Scholarly Coordination
Nunzio Giustozzi

Graphics Coordination
Angelo Galiotto

Editorial Coordination
Cristina Garbagna

Design
Tassinari/Vetta

Page Layout
Elisa Seghezzi

Editing
Gail Swerling

Technical Coordination
Andrea Panozzo

Quality Control
Giancarlo Berti

Translation
Richard Sadleir

Texts
Matteo Cadario
Nunzio Giustozzi
Marta Chiara Guerrieri

Reprint 2017
New Update Edition 2007
First Edition 2004

© Ministero dei Beni e delle Attività Culturali e del Turismo
Soprintendenza Speciale per il Colosseo,
il Museo Nazionale Romano e l'Area Archeologica di Roma

An Editorial Realization by
Mondadori Electa S.p.A., Milano

www.electaweb.com

Contents

The Roman Forum

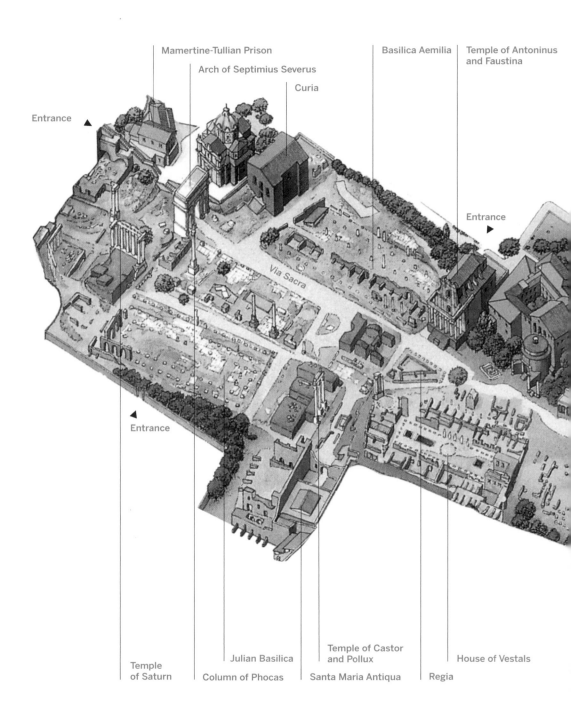

Mamertine-Tullian Prison

Arch of Septimius Severus

Curia

Basilica Aemilia

Temple of Antoninus
and Faustina

Entrance ▲

Entrance ▶

Via Sacra

▲
Entrance

Temple
of Saturn

Julian Basilica

Column of Phocas

Temple of Castor
and Pollux

Santa Maria Antiqua

Regia

House of Vestals

Basilica of Maxentius

Suggestions for a Visit

The Forum is a highly complex site. Its monuments were built in many different periods and were often not all in use at the same time. So visitors are advised to follow a route that is topographical rather than historical. They should begin from the northern area, with access from the street called Via dei Fori Imperiali, then continue in the direction of the Capitol and finally towards the Palatine and the Arch of Titus.

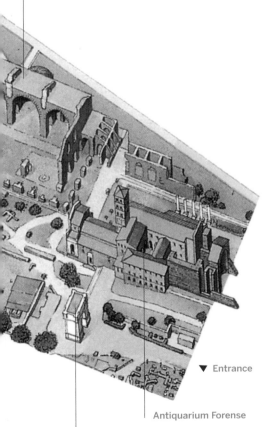

▼ Entrance

Antiquarium Forense

Arch of Titus

Key to Plan

1. Large dedicatory inscription
2. Portico of Caius and Lucius Caesar
3. *Tabernae Novae*
4. Chapel of Venus Cloacina
5. Basilica Fulvia-Aemilia
6. *Lapis Niger*
7. Comitia
8. Curia Iulia
9. Base of the statue of Mars
10. Bases of the columns of Arcadius, Honorius and Theodosius
11. Arch of Septimius Severus
12. Base of column of Costantius II
13. The Decennalia
14. Imperial Rostra
15. Rostra Vandalica
16. Mundus/Umbilicus Urbis
17. Ara Saturni
18. Miliarium Aureum
19. Tabularium
20. Temple of Concord
21. Temple of Vespasian and Titus
22. Temple of the Dei Consentes
23. Temple of Saturn
24. Column of Phocas
25. Inscription of Lucius Naevius Surdinus
26. Fig, olive tree and vine
27. Shafts
28. *Lacus Curtius*
29. *Doliola*
30. Late-ancient *Doliola*
31. Honorary columns
32. Temple of the Diefied Julius
33. *Rostra Divi Iulii*
34. Arch of Augustus (Arch of Actium)
35. Julian Basilica
36. Santa Maria Antiqua
37. Hall in brickwork
38. Horrea Agrippiana
39. Temple of Castor and Pollux
40. *Lacus Iuturnae*
41. Oratory of Quaranta Martiri
42. Temple of Antonino and Faustina
43. Cemetery
44. Private residence
45. Regia
46. Temple of Vesta
47. House of the Vestals
48. Aedicule
49. Domus Publica
50. Temple of Romulus
51. Mediaeval Portico
52. Shrine of Bacchus
53. Basilica of Maxentius
54. Horrea Vespasiani
55. House of M. Aemilius Scaurus
56. Arch of Titus
57. Antiquarium Forense

*The numbers in parentheses
in the texts refer to the numbers
of the monuments on the plan.*

In the Heart of the Ancient City

Long before the Forum became the political hub of the rising city of Rome, far back in the monarchical age (mid-8th century BC), it was a swampy and inhospitable valley, where the inhabitants of the villages on the neighbouring hills (the Palatine, Capitol and Velia) used to bury their dead. Tradition has it that the second king of Rome, Numa Pompilius, established his residence here, but it was with the Etruscan dynasty of the Tarquins that the Forum was paved for the first time, and so gradually became the centre of public life. Most important of all, the Tarquins channelled the Velabrum, the stream that flowed into the valley, making it a swamp, by building the Cloaca Maxima.

On page 14
General view of the Forum
from the Capitol.

Long before the Forum became the political hub of the rising city of Rome, far back in the monarchical age (mid-8th century BC), it was a swampy and inhospitable valley, where the inhabitants of the villages on the neighbouring hills (the Palatine, Capitol and Velia) used to bury their dead. Tradition has it that the second king of Rome, Numa Pompilius, established his residence here, but it was with the Etruscan dynasty of the Tarquins that the Forum was paved for the first time, and so gradually became the centre of public life. Most important of all, the Tarquins channelled the Velabrum, the stream that flowed into the valley, making it a swamp, by building the Cloaca Maxima. It was as a result of these improvements that the Forum became the true centre of the community, the focus of political and religious life in Rome. By the 6th century BC the complex of the Comitia had been built there. Together with the Curia Hostilia, the Comitia was the meeting place of the Roman citizens, senators and magistrates, and it was here that shrines were built for the most ancient religious cults in the city: the temples of Saturn, Vulcan, Mars and Vesta. The second half of the 5th century BC was a very dark period in the history of Rome and consequently for the Forum. Building picked up again, as far as we know in the years following the burning of Rome by the Gauls (traditional date: 390 BC), an episode that was almost certainly exaggerated by the sources, since it has left no archaeological traces.

A more conscious policy of giving the Forum a monumental scale began at the end of the Punic wars (late 3rd-early 2nd century BC.), when Rome, having long spread its rule over the peninsula, came to dominate the whole Mediterranean, extending its trade to the Middle East and beyond. The city's increased political power, the multiplication of contacts and trade, as well as direct knowledge of the great Hellenistic capitals (Alexandria, Pergamum, Antioch, Athens), with their spectacular architecture, created a new sense of urban and architectural space. The result was the construction of major new buildings where economic and legal business could be conducted (the basilicas) and the rebuilding of the archaic shrines on a more monumental scale. In the middle years of the 1st century BC, Caesar built his Forum by demolishing the Comitia and rebuilding the Curia in a position that made it a sort of annex to the *dictator*'s Forum. Subsequently Augustus oversaw various alterations, but his project with the greatest impact on the history of the Forum was the construction, on its east side, of a temple to the deified Caesar (the aedes Divi Iulii). With recognition of the office of Emperor and the construction of other monumental spaces (the Forums of Augustus, Vespasian, Nerva and Trajan) by emperors who left an enduring mark on the city's urban development, the Forum, though remaining the symbolic centre of the Roman State, gradually lost its real political function. Instead it became the setting for the most important rite of legitimisation of the power of the emperors, with their deification after their death (the temple to the deified Caesar and those to Vespasian, Titus and Faustina, and Antoninus Pius).

From this time there followed numerous efforts at restorations and redevelopment, especially after the fires that in different periods destroyed a number of buildings. The last project on a monumental scale was undertaken by Maxentius in the early 4th century AD: from this period the Forum began to decline, and, like the city itself, it was now no longer the centre of the Empire.

Pope Gregory at the Excavations

*Pope Gregory XVI visited the excavations in the Forum on
12 March 1836 and the Diario di Roma recorded his visit the
following day, with lavish praise for the discernment of the
illustrious visitor, offering an easy mark for the mordant
irony of Giuseppe Gioacchino Belli.*

*"Well!," said the Pope when he had a walk
To see the excavations in the Cow Field,
"What a nice ditch! what a nice hole!
A nice cave! Everything so nice!*

*"And just look at that capital
Never saw a better carved with a chisel!
And look at this pepper-stone here:
It's just the thing for a stove!"*

*So while the Pope, surrounded by a score
of architects and antiquarians of his court
was expressing his sage opinions,*

*the crowd, some softly and some out loud
said: "Ah! this saintly man has great talent!
Ah! a Pope of his stature is a great stroke of luck!"
15 March 1836*

The North Side

If you enter the Forum from the square called Largo Romolo e Remo, you have to descend a flight of steps between the Temple of Antoninus and Faustina and the Basilica Aemilia before reaching the level of the ancient Via Sacra, the road that ran east to west through the Forum and was used for the religious processions and celebrations of the triumphal generals on their way to the Capitol.

As you go towards the Capitol along the road, which still retains at many points the paving of the Augustan period, you will find on your right the **Basilica Aemilia** (5). Founded by a member of the *gens* (or clan) Aemilia, from whom it takes its name, this is the sole surviving basilica whose plan still dates from the republican period, though its present appearance is the result of extensive restoration under the empire. This building, like the Julian Basilica on the opposite side of the Forum, was the place where justice was administered, economic and financial transactions took place and the whole business of buying and selling that normally went on in the Forum would be moved indoors in bad weather.

On the side towards the Forum, where the entrances to the basilica were located, all that can be seen is the bases of the columns and some architectural fragments of the portico that Augustus dedicated to Caius and Lucius Caesar (2), his designated successors. On the same side, you can also make out the tabernae that stood in front of the public building. These were a series of small chambers that, literary sources tell us, were occupied by the *argentarii* or money-lenders (3).

At the north-west corner of the Forum stood the buildings that formed the political centre of Rome in the republican period: the **Comitia**, **Curia** and **Rostra**. Very few traces remain of the republican **Comitia** (7), the place of the popular assemblies, because Caesar, when he built his Forum in the area behind it, took over the site for the new Curia Iulia. As we can deduce from what remains of it and from the Comitia of the most ancient Roman colonies, which imitated the Comitia of the mother city, it must have been a circular space surrounded by steps. Nearby there must have stood the more ancient Curia (remains of it have been found beneath the church of Santi Luca e Martina), traditionally attributed to King Tullius Hostilius: here the Senate officially met. The large brick building you now see is the **Curia Iulia** (8), which has been quite well preserved because was transformed into a church in the 8th century. Inside it, despite restoration in the 1930s, the marble floor is original, dating from the time of Diocletian, with stepped sides forming seats for the senators. At the far end there was the statue of Victory, placed there by Augustus. Almost four centuries later St. Ambrose had it removed against the resistance of the last remaining pagan families of Rome.

Detail of the marble frieze that decorated the architrave, discovered in the Basilica Aemilia during excavations: it depicts various episodes of the mythical history of Rome, including the rape of the Sabine maidens, represented here.

The Curia Iulia with, in the foreground, the base of the Decennalia.

Two large carvings, known as the **Plutei of Trajan**, are now placed in the Curia, though they were originally part of a monument in the Forum. They illustrate two episodes of this emperor's reign which actually took place in the Forum. The relief on the left shows the destruction of the registers of debts granted by Trajan, and that on the right the institution of assistance to poor families: in both we find represented in the background the monuments of the south-eastern area of the Forum, from the Temple of Vespasian and Titus to that of Castor and Pollux.

Another place of the greatest importance in Rome's political life was the platform from which the magistrates spoke. It was called the **Rostra** (14), because the *rostra* (or beak-shaped prows) of the enemy fleet destroyed at Antium in 338 BC were placed here to celebrate the victory. The Rostra near the Arch of Septimius Severus , of which all that remains is the brick screen at the front and the pillars on which originally rested a wooden platform, are a reconstruction dating from Augustan times of the more ancient republican platform.

Opposite the Curia there is one of the most ancient and significant monuments in the Forum: the ***Lapis Niger*** (6), an area of the floor that is distinguished from the rest because it is made of black marble and surrounded by a balustrade. In the ancient sources this place is identified with the point where Romulus was killed, or vanished into the sky, depending on the version of the legend, and with the Shrine of Vulcan. Excavations underneath this part of the paving brought to light the remains of a small open shrine, consisting of an altar, the base of a statue and a stone with an inscription in archaic Latin, which can be dated to

The stone with an inscription in archaic Latin, found in the shrine of Vulcan, under the *Lapis Niger*.

Engraving by Giovan Battista Piranesi with the Campo Vaccino.

From Dereliction to Rediscovery

In the centuries of the early Middle Ages the ancient remains were abandoned and forgotten, but they were also preserved by being mostly buried in the ground. The only monuments of the Forum that continued to have a life of their own were buildings that happened to be converted into churches, a process that began in the 6th century AD when the Curia Iulia, became the church of Sant'Adriano, the Temple of Romulus was converted into the church of Santi Cosma e Damiano, a room of the imperial residence into Santa Maria Antiqua, and the Temple of Antoninus and Faustina refashioned to house the church of San Lorenzo in Miranda. Little by little all memory was lost of what the Forum had represented in antiquity, until in the Middle Ages when it was called the Campo Vaccino (Cow Field). Paradoxically, the period when the monuments in the Forum suffered from the greatest depredations was the Renaissance. The revival of building meant that the Forum and its monuments were regarded as an immense quarry of building materials, which were stripped off and carted away. The greatest destruction took place between 1540 and 1550, when work picked up on the building of the basilica of St. Peter. Intellectuals and artists like Raphael and Michelangelo protested unavailingly: buildings that were still almost intact, like the temples of the deified Julius, of Saturn, of Castor and Pollux, etc., were reduced to the state in which we see them today. Hence the saying, "They destroyed the Rome of the Caesars to build the Rome of the Popes." However, late in the 18th century, interest revived in a more scholarly approach to Roman antiquity, but it was only after the unification of Italy that major excavations were conducted in the Forum. The leading archaeologists were Pietro Rosa, Giuseppe Fiorelli, Rodolfo Lanciani and Giacomo Boni, scholars to whom Roman archaeology is deeply indebted. (*M.C.G.*)

middle of the monarchical period (6th century BC.) The inscription is boustrophedic (i.e. written in lines running alternately from right to left or left to right) and, though mutilated, appears to be a sacred law to which even the king had to submit. So it appears that this was an ancient shrine, in all probability dedicated to Vulcan, with whom the religion of the first hero-king of Rome was probably associated at quite an early date.

Today the **Mamertine** or **Tullian prison** lies outside the Forum, but in ancient times it opened onto the *Clivus Argentarius*, another street, famous for money-lenders, which led up from the Forum to the Capitol.

The arch of Septimius Severus.

Arch of Septimius Severus,
detail of the Victory
with trophy on the spandrel
of the arch.

The West Side

The Via Sacra then continues under the majestic **Arch of Septimius Severus** (11). This triumphal arch with three passages is built entirely of marble and was erected by the African emperor in 203 AD to celebrate his victory over the Parthians. On the attic is the dedication to Septimius Severus and his son Caracalla. Among the dedicators there was originally his other son Geta, but his name was cancelled after he was murdered by order of Caracalla himself. The monument is very richly decorated (there are Victories with trophies, the personifications of the seasons, river gods, etc.), but the most original part consists of four panels set above the smaller vaults, representing the principal episodes of two military campaigns in Asia. The representation is arranged in bands set above each other, which should be read from bottom to top. Two of the best preserved panels are those facing the Capitol: in the panel on the right we see the

Roman army attacking an enemy city with siege machinery, the submission of some Parthian tribes and, above, the emperor with his council of war in a fortified camp. In the panel on the left we see the attack on the city of Seleucia on the Tigris and its surrender. The celebration of the emperor and of his military triumphs was originally completed, as we can see on a coin from this period, by a bronze chariot and four horses with the two Severi set above the arch. Next to the southern pillar of the arch is a circular brick structure, called the **Mundus or Umbilicus Urbis** (16). As its same name suggests, it marks the spot that was believed to be the centre of Rome and also the point of contact between the world of the living and the dead: it was therefore symbolically related to the foundation of the city and the rites associated with it. The shorter west side of the Forum, which frames the Capitoline Tabularium, the ancient State Archives built by Sulla, is occupied by sacred buildings erected in different periods. Going from north to south, the first you meet is the **Temple of Concord** (20), which is traditionally said to have been built by Camillus, who had defeated the Volscii at Veii, to mark the end of the conflict between patricians and plebeians with the Sextian-Licinian laws of 367 BC. Today, unfortunately, only the plinth remains, but the splendid architectural decoration preserved in the Tabularium testifies to the importance of this shrine, where the Senate often met. (It was here that Cicero delivered his orations against Catiline.) Tiberius eventually turned it into a sort of museum, placing here many of the original Greek statues that he had brought to Rome on his return from "exile" in Rhodes. Nearby is the **Temple of Vespasian and Titus** (21), built by Domitian for his deified father and brother: at the corner of the podium there remain three Corinthian columns with the architrave above, decorated with the implements used in making sacrifices (the *patera*, or dish, the axe, knife, etc.). Part of the dedicatory inscription can still be seen on it. Also on the slope of the Capitol, between the Forum and the road called the Clivus Capitolinus, is a rather unusual building built on a plan in the form of an obtuse angle, with eight small rooms opening at the sides. The inscription on the trabeation above the columns (which were set up again in the mid-19th century) enables us to identify the complex with the portico of the **Temple of the Dei Consentes** (22), built in the Flavian period over a more ancient shrine from republican times, and restored in the middle of the 4th century AD.

The chambers at the back probably contained cult images of the Dei Consentes, the twelve deities that formed the supreme divine pantheon. In the south-west corner of the Forum rise the slender Ionic columns of the vestibule of the **Temple of Saturn** (23), set on a raised plinth. This was the most ancient shrine of the republican period after the Temple of Capitoline Jupiter, dedicated to the god who, according to myth, was the first ruler of Rome. This building replaced the original place of religion of the deity, a small open shrine from the archaic period, also in the Forum: this was the ***Ara Saturni*** (17), today visible under a shelter opposite the flight of steps. The remains of this temple date from to late 3rd century AD, with the exception of the podium and the avant-corps (the part projecting at the front), which date from the late republican period. The collapse of part of it shows that the avant-corps was empty inside because it housed the Treasury of the Roman state. The base of a column opposite the

The Temple of Saturn and the Arch of Septimius Severus viewed from the Capitol.

Reconstructed drawing
of the preparations for
spectacles at the Forum.

podium of the Temple of Saturn is all that remains of the **Miliarium Aureum** (18), the column erected by Augustus to indicate the ideal point on which converged the major roads of the Empire and on which may have recorded the distances of the principal cities from Rome.

The Middle of the Forum

If you go towards the east, you will have the **middle of the Forum** on your left. This is a large paved space which contains the remains of some late honourary monuments: the column on a stepped base of the Byzantine emperor Phocas (24), the last monument erected in the Forum (608 AD), and the seven columns erected in the Lower Empire on the south side (31).

The three trees sacred to the Romans: the fig, the olive and the vine, which Pliny the Elder tells us grew in the middle of the Forum (26), have been replanted in the unpaved area before the Rostra. In the imperial period these trees replaced the Ficus Ruminalis, the fig tree sacred to the god Faunus, a symbol of fertility and the organization of the state which made a people rich and prosperous.

Immediately to the east of the column of Phocas can be seen, set in the travertine pavement, a large inscription (extensively restored) (25) that commemorates the official who had the paving laid under the reign of Augustus: the urban praetor *Lucius Naevius Surdinus*.

In the middle of the Forum there is an area set below the level of the surrounding pavement, which it has been identified as the **Lacus Curtius** (28), so called because it remained a marsh down to the time of Augustus, when it was drained by sinking a well. The circular base open in the middle on the east side was probably the foundation of the well. Various legends have come down to us about Curtius, the man who gave his name to the monument: one of these relates that he was a Sabine prince who fell with his horse into the *lacus* or marshy abyss. He

The Games in the Forum

Between the Rostra and the *Lacus Curtius* you can still see some pits open in the pavement. Scholars have identified them as a system of tunnels under the Forum used during gladiatorial combats. The *munera* (as the these shows were called in Latin), were held in the Forum down to the reign of Augustus, when the Amphitheatre of Statilius Taurus was built in the Campus Martius.

When the shows were being held, temporary platforms used to be erected round the central space and the system of tunnels was equipped, as happened later in the Flavian amphitheatre, with freight elevators that raised weapons, machinery and whatever else was required for the combats to the level of the arena. (*M.C.G.*)

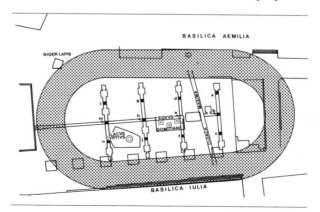

appears in a relief from late republican times found in the vicinity: a cast of it has been placed here. The war between the Romans and Sabines in the reign of Romulus appears in numerous myths about the origins of buildings and cults in the Forum (the Comitia, for example was said to be the place where the leaders of the two tribes met to negotiate peace), but a more likely interpretation is found in Livy, who derived the name from the consul Caius Curtius, who in the mid-5th century BC is said to have delimited an area struck by a bolt of lightning, an omen which in ancient times was considered particularly significant. The east side of the Forum is closed by the **Temple of the Deified Julius** (32), erected by Augustus in 29 BC to mark the deification of Julius Caesar after his death. This was the first time a ruler had ever been deified in Rome. The building suffered badly from depredations over the centuries and today, with the exception of some fragments of the architectural decoration, only the podium remains. Here, in the hemicycle that stood in front of the building, are the remains of an altar commemorating the spot where Caesar was cremated. Subsequently the hemicycle was enclosed with a wall to prevent the cult of Caesar becoming too popular.

On the south side of the temple are the fragmentary remains of a triumphal arch, erected by Augustus to commemorate his victory over Antony and Cleopatra (34). The *rostra* (prows) of the Egyptian ships defeated at Actium were placed on the other oratorical platform, called the *Rostra Divi Iulii* (33), which faces the temple. A second Arch of Augustus, set symmetrically opposite the first on the north side, commemorates his the victory over the Parthians. Set on the same axis as this, to stress the continuity of Roman dominion in the East, Septimius Severus built his arch, again for victory over the Parthians, two centuries later.

The South Side

Between the Temple of Saturn and that of Castor and Pollux, on the south side of the Forum, stood the **Julian Basilica** (35), so-called because it was begun by Caesar and completed by Augustus. It was erected on the site of the Basilica Sempronia, dating from republican times, which in turn—according to ancient sources—was built over the House of Scipio Africanus. Recent probes beneath the centre of the building have brought to light the hall of a residence that archaeologists believe may well be that of Scipio, the general who defeated Hannibal. Today, unfortunately, all that remains of the Julian Basilica is the podium, steps and bases of the columns and pillars: however it was a building of great splendour, according to our sources, and contained four courts of law. Testimony to the life of the past that the visitor should not miss are the graffiti cut into some steps towards the Forum: the so-called *tabulae lusoriae,* meaning the fields for games of draughts, morris, etc., with which idlers whiled away the time. It should be remembered the Forum was not just the arena of business, politics and the administration of justice, but also the place of social focus for the common people of Rome. Between the Julian Basilica and the Temple of Castor and Pollux is the Vicus Tuscus, a street that took its name from an area of shops owned mainly by Etruscans in the neighbouring district of Velabrum. Along the Vicus were ranged shops built in the age of Hadrian on the west side of an enormous chamber built of brick in the reign of Domitian. This site was partly occupied in the 6th century by the church of Santa Maria Antiqua. It is difficult to understand what these buildings were originally: they may have been the chambers of an imperial palace on the Palatine. Recently the large chamber made of brick has been identified as the Temple of Minerva, which the sources place in this zone and where Hadrian founded the **Athenaeum** (37), a sort of academy or university, and where the heirs to the imperial throne also received their education and was the centre of the philhellenic culture that the emperor fostered in Rome. Just south of this there are the remains of the **Horrea Agrippiana** (38), large warehouses built by Agrippa in a district that was prevalently commercial, as is also shown by its position, connecting the Forum and the meat market (Forum Boarium) further towards the Tiber.

The **Temple of Castor and Pollux** (39), of which three great marble columns still stand on their tall plinth, was one of the largest of the period, but it retained

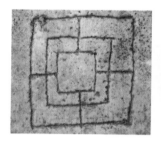

all its prestige even later, after being rebuilt at various times (the last under Tiberius). The cult of the Dioscuri, sons of Jupiter and of Leda, a mortal, was imported to Latium from Greece early of the 5th century BC, almost certainly by the aristocratic party, which made these knightly heroes its patrons. This function is confirmed by legends relating the deeds of Castor and Pollux to a Roman setting. It was said, for example, that two mysterious knights led the Romans to victory in the battle of Lake Regillus against the Latins (499 BC) and they were seen watering their horses in the spring of Juturna, after announcing victory to the city before disappearing. As often happened in Rome, the temple was not just the centre of a cult. As we know from literary sources, in this sanctuary the Senate met on various occasions, but it also housed the office of weights and measures and contained a number of money-lending booths, probably in the small rooms in the podium. The myth of the Dioscuri is also associated with the **Juturna Spring** (40) the most important in the city in the early republican period. Traditionally Juturna was considered a nymph, the sister of King Turnus. The spring flowed into a monumental marble basin, just to the east of the Temple of Castor and Pollux, probably installed by Lucius Aemilius Paulus. To this general, who conquered Greece and defeated Perseus of Macedon in 168 BC, we also owe the statues of two heroes on horseback, found as fragments in the basin and now preserved in the Antiquarium. The statues of the two knights must originally have been set on the pedestal at the centre of the spring, since legend related that the Dioscuri appeared for the second time near the spring, when they brought news of the victory of Aemilius Paulus over Perseus. A little to south is the shrine in the form of an aedicule to the goddess Juturna, rebuilt in the reign of Trajan. It is set at an angle to the buildings nearby, perhaps reflecting the position of a road of which all trace has been lost.

The East Side

Since they are now regarded as forming a single complex, the monuments that follow will be treated as part of the Roman Forum even though, according to the division into districts (*regiones*) carried out by Augustus, the whole area between the Basilica Aemilia and the Temple of Venus and Rome no longer formed part of the Forum. In the same way, the whole area south of the Via Sacra starting from the House of the Vestals was considered already to be part of the Palatine *regio*. The complex of irregular shape to the north of the Temple of Vesta has been identified as the **Regia** (45), the residence of the king in the monarchical period: according to legend, it was originally the house of the second king of Rome, Numa Pompilius. Excavation of building has, in fact, turned up a fragment of a pot in *bucchero* pottery, dating from the mid-6th century BC, with the word *rex* carved on it. In addition, the remains of the architectural decoration, including a pottery slab depicting the head of a bull, show this was an especially important residence, perhaps part of the dwelling of the dynasty of the Tarquins. With the transition to the Roman republic it most likely became the seat of the *rex Sacrorum*, the official who replaced the king in his religious functions, but when it was last rebuilt in the archaic period the building retained the same plan and features down to the imperial period: a sign of the sacred respect paid to it.

Interpretation of the remains is unfortunately very difficult because of the poor state of preservation of the complex. The building seems, however, to comprise two parts: to the south is a rectangular area divided into three chambers, which have been identified as the sanctuary of Ops, the goddess of harvests, and that of Mars, the divine ancestor of Romulus. To the north is a spacious courtyard which was originally arcaded.

The **Temple of Antoninus and Faustina** (42), just north of the Regia, has survived because it was converted into the church of San Lorenzo in Miranda, but the big holes in the blocks of tuff (a volcanic stone) covering the podium show that the marble that originally faced this building was stripped off and carted away in the 15th-16th centuries. The temple was built by the emperor Pius Antoninus for his deified wife Faustina, and later, after his death, dedicated to him as well. It is a temple set on a raised plinth with a flight of steps. Though restored using brick in modern times, it still preserves in the middle the base of an altar, since– it should be borne in mind– in Greece and Rome the altar where the rites were celebrated was usually placed outside and not inside sacred buildings. Finally note on the two longer sides of the cell a frieze, very well preserved, decorated with gryphons and vegetable motives.

East of this temple there is another small temple built on a round plan. It is in an excellent state of preservation because it was turned into the vestibule of the church of Santi Cosma e Damiano behind it. A noteworthy detail is the bronze portal, part of the original decoration of the temple, which goes back to the early

Architectural slab from the Regia: clearly visible is the figure of the Minotaur, an allusion to the myth of Theseus, the hero who, through his enterprise and with divine favour was invested with regal powers.

The Temple of Antoninus and Faustina.

4th century AD. Mediaeval sources state this was a **Temple dedicated to Romulus** (50), son of Maxentius, but today there is evidence that it was originally the Temple of Jupiter Stator, rededicated by Maxentius to his son who had died young. The building was eventually converted back by Constantine into a temple for the cult of Jupiter and the Penates, the Romans' household gods. Another sign of the various phases of construction that affected the Forum is the **Mediaeval Portico** (51) made of brick that follows the Temple of Romulus.

The north-eastern part of the Forum, with the hill called the Velia, is dominated by the imposing brick volume of the **Basilica of Maxentius** (53), of which, unfortunately, only the north aisle survives. The building was begun by Maxentius in the early years of the 4th century AD on a site previously occupied by the Horrea Piperataria (spice warehouses) dating from the Flavian period. When Constantine defeated Maxentius at the Milvian bridge he completed the building, partly altering the original design. The basilica consisted of a nave with side aisles set on an east-west axis: the nave was originally supported by eight columns of *proconnesio* marble. (The only surviving column was moved in 1613 by Pope Paul V to the square of Santa Maria Maggiore, where it still stands.) By contrast, the side aisles consisted of three areas covered with massive coffered barrel vaulting. The original axis of the building shows that the entrance was at the eastern end, so probably the statue of the emperor was set in the large apse that opened out on the west side. Sure enough, in the 15th century a colossal statue of Constantine was found here.

Detail of the frieze on the architrave of the Temple of Antoninus and Faustina, watercolor by J.-F. Ménager (1783–1864). École Nationale Supérieure des Beaux-Arts, Paris.

This was an acrolith, a statue with only the exposed parts made of marble. Today they are preserved in the courtyard of the Palazzo dei Conservatori on the Capitol. In a later period, however, the project was altered, perhaps again by Constantine. The main axis of the building was changed to north-south, and on the south side, towards the Forum, a more monumental entrance was added, consisting of a portico with four large porphyry columns and a flight of steps to make good the difference in height between the Via Sacra and the Velia. Aligned with the new entrance an apse was built into the opposite wall, in which were set various niches with statues, of which unfortunately nothing remains. Starting in the late 4th century AD, the Basilica of Maxentius formed the meeting place for some of the most important institutions of Rome: the *Praefectura Urbi*, which replaced the consulate of the republican and imperial periods, and the *Secretarium Senatus*, the senatorial court, which moved from the Curia Iulia into the apse in the north nave of the basilica. (*M.C.G.*)

Bronze portal
of the Temple of Romulus.

The Basilica of Maxentius,
detail of the lacunaries that
decorate the barrel vault.

The Basilica of Maxentius.

The Mamertine – Tullian Prison: The Descent to Hades

There are numerous descriptions of the Tullian keep. That by Calpurnius Flaccus is sadly true to life: "I saw the public prison built of massive stones, which receives just a little light from narrow openings. Through them the most wretched prisoners see the Robur and the Tullianum and every time the creaking of the iron door wakes them, they feel they are dying and by witnessing each other's tortures learn what awaits them. The lash whistles through the air, food is forced into the throats of those who refuse it by the dirty hands of the executioner ... The filth torments their bodies, the chains cut into their hands."

On the slopes of the Capitol, between the Roman Forum and the Forum of Caesar, under the church of San Giuseppe dei Falegnami, begins the descent to a fearsome underground world. Built, according to tradition, by Ancus Marcius (640–616 BC) in the middle of the city and on a dominant position to terrorize the ever-more numerous criminals, the most ancient and notorious prison of Rome was called the Mamertine in the Middle Ages, after the Sabine god Mamers (Mars), who was believed to have a temple in the neighbourhood. The present building is only part of the original complex, which extended towards the citadel with other chambers set in caves hewn out of the volcanic stone. On the flight of steps called the Scalae Gemoniae, which still connect the valley of the Forum to the hilltops, the corpses of executed criminals were exhibited to public insult. The location of the prison is not casual: historical sources relate that here, whenever a triumph was celebrated, before the victor began his ascent to the Temple of Capitoline Jupiter, prisoners in his train were led out from the procession to be thrown into the prison and then barbarically killed or left to die. Jugurtha, king of Numidia, starved to death here in 104 BC, Vercingetorix, king of the Gauls, was beheaded in 49 BC, and Sejanus, the minister of Tiberius, was beheaded in 31 AD. These are just some of the eminent names recorded on one of the plaques beside the entrance to the upper cell, while the other provides a list of the Christian martyrs.

There is, however, no evidence that St. Peter and St. Paul were ever held in this prison, as maintained by mediaeval tradition, which also related that it was transformed into oratory called of San Pietro in Carcere, the first place of Christian worship in the Forum.

You enter the complex by descending a flight of steps by the façade, made of blocks of travertine, built closer to the more ancient one in the early imperial period by the consuls whose names are recorded in the large votive inscription. Through an open passage added in modern times we enter a room built on a trapezoidal plan with barrel vaulting in blocks of tuff (a volcanic stone) in the 2nd century BC and enriched in the 18th century by an altar that has two reliquary busts representing Peter and Paul.

This was the true and actual *carcer*, the place where the prisoners were held, and lowered through a trapdoor—once the only entrance—to the cell below to be tortured. This was the most ancient and secret part of the prison, the Tullianum: a name related to the presence of a spring of water (*tullus*) inside it, but also said to derive from the Etruscan king Servius Tullius, who may have built as a cistern here. The cell was originally circular, with walls built entirely of blocks of *peperino* without cement and a *tholos* vault like the Treasury of Atreus at Mycene. Today the ceiling has been lowered, making it more oppressive. It was dark and dank, being always covered with a film of water that stagnated and gave off a foul smell. Hence Jurgurtha's sarcastic exclamation when he was flung naked into the abyss: "Your baths are cold, Romans!" An iron door conceals the opening of a sewer that, flowing into the Cloaca Maxima, carries into the Tiber the waters that collect in the well. The wellhead projects from the modern floor made of brickwork laid in a herringbone pattern. A romantic legend has it that, beyond the door, was a subterranean channel that carried away the dismembered bodies of executed criminals on their journey to the underworld, happy to leave these stones of human cruelty. As if in a symbolic triumph over the cries of the desperate, the Christian tradition sees this as the place where Peter performed the miracle of making water gush from the floor of the prison to christen the prisoners he had converted, as depicted in the bronze relief on the altar in the wall, next to the column, to which the saint is said to have been chained. Giovan Battista Piranesi was fascinated by the prison: here, beneath these looming masses, barely illuminated by a torch, in a frenzy of inspiration he drew his imaginary *Prisons*: nightmarish visions of deep shafts, hanging beams, staircases rising in cramped spaces and ending in the stifling claustrophobia evoked with such mastery in Poe's *The Pit and the Pendulum*. (*N.G.*)

Detail of the relief set on the balustrade of the church of San Giuseppe ai Falegnami, which represents Saints Peter and Paul in the prison.

Santa Maria Antiqua:
A Museum of Early Mediaeval
Roman Painting

Interior of the church
of Santa Maria Antiqua.

The gradual Christianisation of the Forum appears in the church of Santa Maria Antiqua (36). In the first half of the 6th century AD it was laid out in part of the interior (a hall with a quadri-portico, which may have been one of the state rooms) of the imperial palace where it backed onto the western slopes of the Palatine Hill. When Belisarius recaptured Rome from the Goths, this area became the main point of access to the hill where he established the headquarters of the Byzantine government. The buildings erected by Domitian had been transformed, with the portico in front converted into a narthex, when the cult of the Virgin Mary was first estab-

lished, as in the palaces erected by Constantine, where the lobby was often consecrated to the Virgin. The portico running round the sides was converted into an interior with a nave and side aisles and pillars were replaced with columns to create a clear basilica form with an apse in the central wall at the end and small open chapels set in the side aisles.

The church was buried by a landslide in 847 and the shrine of the Virgin was moved to Santa Maria Nova on the Velia Hill, where it occupied the Temple of Venus and Rome. The church was only rediscovered in the last century. The structure and the early mediaeval frescoes were fully restored recently. The part on the right of the present apse of the church is stratified like a palimpsest, where we can identify traces of four successive layers of decoration. The most ancient image, *Mary as Queen of Heaven with Child and an Angel*, was painted immediately after the Byzantine conquest of Rome (first half of the 6th century), as if to stress the change in the administration of the palace. At that time the chamber was used as a guardroom. The markedly Byzantine character of the paintings (confirmed by the pres-

Santa Maria Antiqua, the wall with layers of decoration.

ence of Eastern martyrs and inscriptions in Greek) appear in the iconic, frontal representation typical of the art of Constantinople together with the deliberate use of line to give a distinctive character to the faces, determine the planes and create a sense of depth, in a way earlier adopted in the mosaic in the apse of the nearby basilica of Santi Cosma e Damiano.

This fresco was painted over with an *Annunciation*, of which there still remain part of the Virgin's face and the figure of the angel, popularly known as *Angelo bello*. This shows the hand of a more refined artist and greater freedom in the use of colour and vibrantly expressive effects of light. This painting dates back to 565-578 when the hall became the Palatine church. It is the first signs of the direct and deliberate renewal of the Hellenistic pictorial tradition, which the Graeco-Oriental artists continued represent, much more than the Romans. This happy period was short-lived: the depiction of *The Fathers of the Church* on the same wall already appears much more conventional and rigid. This has been dated to the period of Martin I (649–655), who had the presbytery redecorated. The paintings commissioned by the Greek pope John VII (705-707) are very complex in their iconography and feature a markedly linear quality. He had the arch of the apse redecorated with angels adoring Christ on the cross. The other walls were also decorated with frescos at different times. In the left aisle there is a painting of a row of saints of the Greek and Latin Church with Christ in the middle. Above them is a series of scenes from the Old Testament, of which the stories of Joseph are the least damaged. Well preserved are also the spaces of the *schola cantorum*, with fragments of fresco on the columns and seats, where numerous fragments of early mediaeval sculpture have been placed.

Crucifixion, fresco in the chapel of Theodotus in Santa Maria Antiqua.

Roman art of the 8th century is represented by the frescos of Theodotus (to the left of the presbytery), which date from the period of Pope Zacharias (741-782), represented, together with the donor and his family, in the votive panel. The decoration of the chapel with scenes from the lives of Saints Quiricus and Julitta is dominated on the end wall by a *Crucifixion*. This reveals that the late Hellenistic influences from Constantinople were being replaced by a style of painting that narrated the scenes more rapidly, using drawing to express the movements of the figures and outline the forms and fields of colour, laid on simple and effectively. This very immediate and expressive painting also reflects significant Eastern influences of distant Syrian-Palestinian origin, as in the unusual detail of the long garment worn by Christ.

Also related to the transformation of the church of Santa Maria Antiqua and the Christianisation of the ancient cult of the nymph Juturna in the spring nearby is the **oratory** of the **Quaranta Martiri** (41). The apse is decorated with a large painting from the 8th century: it celebrates the devotion of the soldiers condemned to die in the frozen waters of a lake in Armenia during Diocletian's persecution. The interior has a square plan and still preserves on the right-hand wall a fresco of St. Anthony the Hermit and a marble floor made of fragments from the mediaeval period. (*N.G.*)

Around the Sacred Fire of Vesta

At the point where the Forum begins to rise towards the Palatine, the hearth in the House of the King had become the perpetual fire burning in the **Temple of Vesta** (46), the patron goddess of the community, and symbolising the eternal life of Rome. The building, which is circular, like the most ancient straw-and-wicker huts of Latium, with a hole in the middle of the conical roof to let out the smoke, was predictably burnt down several times and was faithfully rebuilt using different materials, as shown by our sources, which are mainly carvings and coins.

The round Temple of Vesta.

House of the Vestals,
view of the courtyard.

It finally acquired its present appearance when it was restored by Julia Domna, wife of the emperor Septimius Severus in the late 2nd century AD. The remains, restored in the thirties, enable us to understand that the cylindrical cell was decorated with projecting hemi-columns on both interior and exterior; while the temple was enlarged by resting the outer Corinthian columns (with the characteristic fluting filled in at the bottom) on bases detached from the podium and perhaps united by a bronze grate that has now disappeared. The recomposed fragments of the frieze show it was carved with objects used in the cult and ritual of sacrifice: horses' tails, mirrors, olive branches and *bucrani* (representations of the skulls of sacrificial animals), also shows that the architecture was embellished with very refined decorations. However, the cell, entered by steps on the east side, was unusual in not containing a statue of the deity, who was evoked by the perpetual flame. An underground chamber, inaccessible to the profane, contained the objects that Aeneas, according to legend, had brought from Troy, including the magic Palladium. a small archaic image of Athene-Minerva, the pledge of the universal dominion promised to Rome. An image of Vesta was, however, probably placed in the **Ionic Aedicule** dating from the reign of Hadrian, set near the entrance of the **House of the Vestals** (47). These were priestesses consecrated to the ancestral cult, pure and noble, of the goddess. The priestesses were chosen by lot by the *pontifex maximus*: they were six virgins, between the ages of six and ten years old, from patrician families and free from physical imperfections, who served for thirty years with the duty of chastity. The ceremony of investiture was highly picturesque: the maidens' hair was cut off (and hung on a lotus tree) and they put on a white veil that hung over their shoulders and a kind of woollen diadem divided into six cords. The vestals grew up in a kind of modern convent, laid out around a courtyard-garden surrounded by porticos along which were ranged the rooms, while a kitchen, a mill, an oven and a vegetable plot made the house self-sufficient. Responsible for the ritual harvest and preparation of the bread used in sacrifices, the priestesses did not, however, lead a cloistered life. In fact they enjoyed absolute privileges: they were accompanied by the lectors, like the supreme magistrates, had special seats at the public shows, and so great was the respect paid them that if a man condemned to death encountered one on the day of his execution he would be pardoned. But if a vestal broke her vow of chastity she was buried alive in a field, while if inadvertently one of them allowed the sacred fire they constantly tended to go out, she would be publicly flogged: terrible punishments for young women robbed of their childhood.

When her ministry ended, the vestal was, however, able to decide calmly, given her high social position, to marry, choosing among a crowd of suitors or preferring a career. Today only a few sections of the luxurious *domus* can be visited: the courtyard, with fountains and plants that flower in spring, surrounded by statues representing the principal vestals, set at the head of the religious order, whose virtues are described in the inscriptions on the pedestals. The place still preserves the sense of quiet and seclusion which in ancient times protected the priestesses from the turmoil of the city around them. (*N.G.*)

House of the Vestals, north portico with statues of the most important vestals.

The Antiquarium Forense: Rediscovering an Ancient Museum

Antiquarium Forense,
view of Room I.

In some rooms on the first and of second floor laid out around the very fine cloister of the convent of Santa Francesca Romana, which stands on the site of the Temple of Venus in Rome, the archaeologist Giacomo Boni founded an Antiquarium (57) in 1900. Here he brought together and exhibited the most important finds from excavations in the Forum. The whole collection is at present being reorganised. A statue in Greek marble of Aesculapius with a boy in the act of sacrificing a cock, which comes from the Lacus Iuturnae, welcomes the visitor to the entrance on the ground floor, the only part of the museum that can be seen at present. Rooms I-V, which contain materials from the burial grounds and votive wells dating from the archaic period, fortunately preserves the original display unchanged: a rare example of the museological principles of the period. In the middle of Room I, for example, is a model of the cemetery found near the Temple of Antoninus and Faustina and a reconstruction of some of the graves. Around the walls are photos of excavations, drawings of reconstructions, cross-sections of the Forum, etc. In the original display cases, still arranged in good order, are the various grave furnishings. Also noteworthy, in Room II, are the burials in tree trunks of children in the last period when the Forum was used as a cemetery (in the mid-8th and 7th centuries BC), when imported Greek pottery, or imitations of it, reveal contacts with the Greek colonies founded in Italy.

Most of the exhibits of historical and artistic interest are unfortunately contained in the section of the Antiquarium not yet been reopened to the public. We shall examine the most significant in chronological order. The first is a marble head carved in rather severe style (mid-5th century BC), whose workmanship suggests it was made in one of the towns of Magna Graecia. It may have been attached to a body of different material. Outstanding for the softness of the flesh tones is the fragmentary group of the Dioscuri with their horses, from the Juturna spring, which can be dated to the 2nd century BC, though severe in style. Of exceptional importance are the fragments of the large marble frieze, dating from the late republican period and clearly inspired by Hellenistic models, which originally decorated the central hall of the Basilica Aemilia. It recounts the mythical episodes of the origins of Rome: the construction of the wall of Lavinius, the rape of the Sabine maidens, the punishment of Tarpeia and scenes of battle. Finally there are the base and figured capital of a column in an excellent state of preservation from the Temple of Concord in its Tiberian phase, with paired rams that seem about to spring out from the corners. (*N.G.*)

In Honour of Titus, "Delight of Humankind"

The Arch of Titus
after the recent cleaning.

The Arch of Titus, before the
19th century restoration,
in a painting by A.L.R. Ducros
(1748–1810). Musée Cantonal
des Beaux-Arts, Lausanne.

At the point where you go up from the Forum toward the Palatine, the **Arch of Titus** (56), gleaming white after its recent cleaning, now rises up from its foundations, uncovered because the present road level is lower than that of the ancient Via Sacra. The arch owes its partial preservation to its incorporation into the mediaeval fortifications by the Frangipane family. Its single passage was turned into a large portal and the brackets of the gates seriously damaged the decorations. Its present integrity is the result of thorough archaeological restoration by Valadier in the 1820s, recorded in the inscription on the side of the arch facing the Forum. The architect made good the missing parts of the attic and the piers. For the first time he adopted two principles that have become fundamental rules of modern restoration: he differentiated the new materials from the old (travertine as against the noble *pentelico* marble used by the Romans) so as to make the original materials conspicuous, and he simplified the forms in the mouldings of the

orders, whose volumes he merely indicated. In this way Valadier achieved a chromatic and tactile coherence in his restoration, based on a correct interpretation of the architecture of the building. It was Domitian, the last emperor of the Flavian dynasty, who erected the arch in memory of his brother Titus, already deified (after 81 AD), to commemorate his feats and above all his victory in the Jewish war of 70–71 AD, under the reign of their father Vespasian. This is stated in the original dedication carved on the side facing the Coliseum in the attic surmounting the trabeation above the single passage, which is flanked on both fronts by four fluted hemi-columns with composite capitals (Ionic-Corinthian).

The sculptures that decorate the arch are among the most attractive achievements of Roman art. A quick glance suffices to appreciate the small continuous frieze on the outside, which represents the whole triumphal procession in popular style, and the elegant archivolts with winged Victories hovering above a globe with the symbols of glory. In the centre of the elaborate coffered vaulting, a relief represents the Apotheosis of Titus, who rises to heaven on an eagle, while two large side panels illustrate the climax of his triumph. Against a background of the *fasces* carried by the lictors, here arranged confusedly to create a sense of the crowds at the celebration, appears the imperial *quadriga* or four-horse chariot with Titus crowned by Victory, followed by the personifications of the Roman People (bare to the waist) and the Senate (wearing togas), while the goddess Rome controls the horses with a bit. Opposite this is another relief which depicts the earlier moment when the procession is about to pass through the Porta

Triumphalis, set in the Forum Boarium, where the triumph began. The Roman soldiers, crowned with laurel, carry the sacred spoils ransacked from the Temple of Jerusalem and here presented as symbols of the Jewish religion (the silver trumpets, the golden table of the shewbread with the Ark of the Covenant, and the *menorah*, the famous seven-branched candlestick, subsequently lost), while the tables with handles probably held the objects, or mentioned the cities conquered, or actually had painted scenes of salient episodes of the war. A historical document of exceptional importance, the relief testifies to a radical revival of Roman art characterised by the search for a more tactile colouring, effects of light and chiaroscuro, and a spatial dynamism in the forms which are distributed on multiple planes of representation. The sinuous handling of perspective creates the impression that the procession is approaching us in the middle of the scene and then it immediately seems to wind away, giving an unusual sense of movement that culminates in the illusionistic opening of the Triumphal Arch. (*N.G.*)

Portrait of Titus. Capitoline Museums, Rome. The emperor, after a troubled start, succeeded, during his short reign (79–81 AD) in adopting a political line of moderation and mildness. For example, he personally undertook the reconstruction of the cities destroyed by the eruption of Vesuvius and inaugurated the Coliseum with a hundred days of festivities that left a good memory of his rule.

Arch of Titus, inside the passage and a panel that depicts the procession entering the Porta Triumphalis bearing booty from Solomon's temple.

The Forum between the 6th and 9th Centuries

Early mediaeval frescoes
preserved in a niche
in the Curia Iulia,
forming part of the decoration
of the church of Sant'Adriano.

Extensive excavation in the Roman Forum in the late 19th and early 20th century unfortunately has confused our understanding of the later topography of the area in the Middle Ages, since it left very few records of the structures and of the stratigraphy of this period.

As far as we can reconstruct its later history, the Forum seems to have remained substantially the same at least down to the Sack of Rome by the Visigoths under Alaric in 410. It is only after this event that we have records of alterations and restoration of some of its buildings, but there was no change in their functions from the classical period. Partly from literary sources (Procopius, Cassiodorus, etc.), throughout the 6th century and well into the 7th the Roman Forum retained its monumentality, and therefore its prestige, due to its powerful symbolic associations. After this time it began to change gradually. New commercial buildings appeared, such as the shops that backed onto the "columns of honour," and some civil buildings were converted into churches (the most important being Santa Maria Antiqua), as happened to the Curia, which was dedicated to Sant'Adriano in the middle of the following century.

It was in the 7th century that the most far-reaching changes occurred, significantly coinciding with the political and religious events. The founding of workshops to reuse the metals and marble stripped from the classical monuments shows that many buildings, once essential to the city, were no longer felt to be very important.

The role of the Church also became more central to Rome's civil life. The 8th century saw the creation of five *diaconie* in the churches of the Forum: these were charitable organisations which looked after the welfare of the needy. Their work may be reflected in the granaries and wells discovered in the vicinity, as well as a small spa set in the House of the Vestals and probably connected with the church of Santa Maria Antiqua.

The foundation of important religious institutions in this area obviously led to an increase of building in the neighbourhood. This settlement was, however, changed radically in the second half of the 9th century, when a series of natural disasters struck the city, such as an earthquake and flood in 847. In the troubled period that followed, no attempt was made to clear away the accumulated rubble and mud or to repair the damaged sewers, which were abandoned. These events caused the lowest areas to revert to swamp, so that roads and buildings areas had to built up higher. Soon after this the area attracted some fine residences, belonging in all probability to the aristocracy of the period. At this time there were still craft workshops and businesses run by tradesmen in various parts of the Forum. (*M.C.G.*)

The Palatine
and the Circus
Maximus

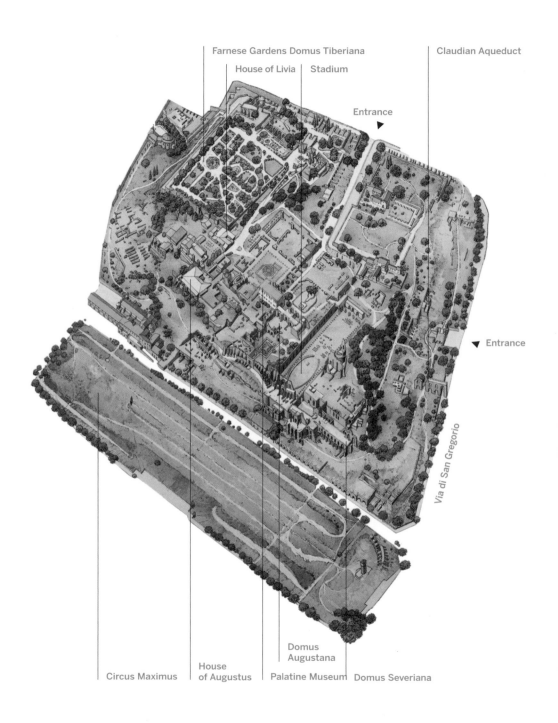

Farnese Gardens Domus Tiberiana

House of Livia Stadium

Claudian Aqueduct

Entrance

Entrance

Via di San Gregorio

Circus Maximus

House of Augustus

Domus Augustana

Palatine Museum Domus Severiana

Suggestions for a Visit

A good point to begin the visit is the area
near the Arch of Titus, from which you
climb up the hill. The route suggested will,
as far as possible, guide you through
chronologically and architecturally
different areas, so that you form a clear idea
of the historical changes and the
development of the monuments. The poor
state of preservation of many of the
buildings on the Palatine gives you just
a glimpse of what must have been the most
important hill in Rome, but the atmosphere
that surrounds it, set amid monumental
ruins and extensive green spaces,
is certainly very moving.

Key to Plan

1. Arch of Titus
2. Plinth
3. Via Sacra
4. Via Nova
5. Clivus Palatinus
6. Porticus Margaritaria
7. Foundations from the Neronian period
8. Domus
9. Shops
10. Arch
11. Plinth of a temple
12. Scalae Caci
13. Romulean huts
14. Cisterns
15. Temple of Magna Mater
16. Auguratorium
17. Brick structures
18. Archaic wall
19. House of Livia
20. House of Augustus
21. Temple of Apollo
22. Domus Tiberiana
23. Neronian cryptoporticus
24. Brick chambers
25. Bath
26. Clivus Victoriae
27. Atrium Gai
28. Domus Flavia
29. Domus Augustana
30. Stadium
31. Casa dei Grifi
32. Aula Isiaca
33. Baths of Livia
34. Brick structures
35. Severian arches
36. Severian baths
37. Baths of Maxentius
38. Septizodium
39. Pedagogium
40. Schola Praeconum
41. Claudian aqueduct
42. Baths of Elegabalus
43. Temple (of the Sun?)
44. Pentapylum
45. Church of San Sebastiano
46. Church of San Bonaventura

*The numbers in parentheses
in the texts refer to the numbers
of the monuments on the plan.*

On the Hill of Romulus and the Caesars

The Palatine is closely associated more than any other part of Rome with legends of the city's foundation. When Aeneas fled from Troy he eventually arrived in Latium, where he was said to have been made welcome by King Evandrus on this hill, while the basket holding Romulus and Remus is said to have been carried by the waters of the Tiber to a cave, later called the Lupercal, on the slopes of the Palatine, where they were suckled by a she-wolf. Later literary sources suggest that the city founded by Romulus was confined essentially to this hill, where Romulus himself dwelt in a house later identified with a hut at the south-west corner of the hill, which was continually restored and rebuilt in honour of the city's mythical founder.

On page 58
Casa dei Grifi, detail of the decoration of an earlier wall with cube patterns in perspective with "lacquered" faces.

The rescue of Romulus and Remus and the demoniac and theological system of the Lupercal. Reconstruction by A. Carandini.

Model of one of the Iron Age huts (8th century BC) excavated on the Palatine (reconstruction by A. Davico, 1950). Palatine Museum, Rome.

Excavations of the lower level of the Domus Augustana conducted in the thirties.

As often happens, the myth and the legend have a historical foundation, as revealed by excavations conducted on the Palatine since the late 19th century. At the very point where tradition put the Casa Romuli (or hut of Romulus), archaeologists have brought to light a village of huts that enable us to date the permanent occupation of the hill to the 8th century BC.

The position of the Palatine, protected by steep rocks and close to the river, made it well suited for permanent settlement.

Memories of the antiquity of the site and legends about it gave the hill that character of holiness that always surrounded it. In the archaic period, literary sources, confirmed by archaeological finds, record above all the existence of cults and religious festivals of ancient tradition, including the festival of the *Lupercalia*, in which wolf-priests, dressed in goatskins, would run about striking married women with thongs in a fertility rite.

This sacred and mythical character was clearly one of the reasons why Augustus built his palace on the hilltop next to the Casa Romuli; close by it he built the Temple of Apollo, his patron god. He clearly meant to enhance the legitimacy of the imperium by presenting himself as the second founder of Rome. Augustus, who was born on the slopes of the hill, purchased the *domus* of the well-known orator Quintus Hortensius Hortalus and gradually extended it by acquiring other residences nearby. In the late republican period the Palatine had also become a select residential district, where many members of Rome's ruling class lived. Excavations have brought to light at various points the remains of these residences (the most ancient is the Casa dei Grifi), which were almost obliterated by construction of the imperial palaces.

Tiberius was the first to plan a monumental residence, the Domus Tiberiana. He was followed by Nero, who built here his first residence, the Domus Transitorius, and part of the Domus Aurea. It was, however, Domitian who created the dynastic palace par excellence: this was a wholly new architectural model, consisting of a self-enclosed complex, where the

public part and the private were kept sharply separate for the first time, so allowing the emperor to appear to his subjects in a hieratic light, aloof from the rest of the world. The subsequent extensions of the imperial *domus*, above all by the Severians, followed and perfected this model and contributed progressively to its codification, to the point where in late antiquity the hill's Latin name, Palatium, became synonymous with palace.

The last large work on the Palatine was, it appears, the Temple of the Sun, built by Elagabalus, the last but one of the Severian emperors. After this, new construction on the hill slowed, heralding the slow decline that followed the transfer of the capital of the Empire to Constantinople. The Palatium formally remained an imperial palace but gradually lost the political significance it had had for more than ten centuries.

We have little information about the Palatine hill in the Middle Ages. Besides being the occasional residence of emperors and popes, in the 11th and 12th centuries much of the Palatine was converted into a stronghold by the Frangipane, one of the most important Roman families of the period. After a further period of dereliction, in the Renaissance the hill was repopulated, with the creation of gardens, villas and vineyards owned by noble Roman families (the Farnese, Barberini, Mattei, etc.), but it was this that led to the depredation and dispersal of its riches.

The Clivus Palatinus

The best way to reach the Palatine is by its northern slopes, where an ancient road, the **Clivus Palatinus** (5), climbs up from the Arch of Titus. The visitor will see immediately on his right a series of brick walls, identified as the remains of a monumental arcaded structure

History of the Excavations

The Renaissance, it is true, saw a revival of interest in antiquity but it was also the period when the desire to possess treasures of ancient art got the upper hand in most cases over a desire to understand the past better. The conversion of the Palatine to vineyards and gardens revealed the remains of the imperial palace and its decorations: then followed excavations aimed only at recovering works of art. This was ruinous because it permanently destroyed not only ancient materials but also valuable historical and topographical information. These excavations continued for centuries until finally Pietro Rosa was appointed by Napoleon III, the new owner of the Farnese Gardens, to direct excavations on the whole of the Palatine and introduced a more correct method of research. Pietro Rosa was also the first to stop the systematic dispersal of the works discovered by founding an Antiquarium on the Palatine, the forerunner of the present one. Finally, with the unification of Italy, research was taken in hand by eminent scholars: Rodolfo Lanciani, Giacomo Boni and Alfonso Bartoli laid the foundations of a knowledge of the Palatine and its monuments which is still increasing today thanks to excavations by the Archaeological Service of Rome. (*M.C.G.*)

which had a commercial function (known as the **Porticus Margaritaria**) (6). Continuing the ascent, a modern ramp, also on the right, leads the visitor to the monumental entrance of the Orti Farnesiani or Farnese Gardens, laid out in the 16th century over the Domus Tiberiana, almost entirely obliterating it.

The Domus Tiberiana

The first imperial palace on the Palatine was built by Tiberius and later extended towards the Forum by Caligula, completely restructured by Nero and again, for the last time, by Domitian. Today the only remaining signs of all this splendour are the imposing arched structures that flank the Roman Forum (22). Of the central area, which once occupied almost the whole west side of the hill, all that is visible now are the substructures, on which the Farnese gardens were laid out.

This palace has not yet been entirely explored, but recent studies have suggested that Nero's rebuilding consisted in creating a large platform which provided the substructure for a central pavilion flanked by other pavilions, separated from each other by large areas of garden. Nero also bounded the platform with a cryptoporticus (or underground gallery) running along the east side. Excavation of this cryptoporticus has recovered the remains of mosaics on the floors, with paintings and polychrome stucco decorations on the walls, of which some examples are visible today in the Palatine Museum.

Earthenware head of a deity, perhaps Zeus (early 3rd century BC), from the site of the Temple of Victory, near that of Magna Mater. Palatine Museum, Rome.

Earthenware head of Apollo, from the Domus Tiberiana. Palatine Museum, Rome.

Excavations of the lower level of the Domus Augustana conducted in the thirties.

The South-West Zone

After walking through the Farnese Gardens and the Domus Tiberiana, you reach the south-west zone of the hill, which has some of the most ancient remains of the Palatine.

On the west and north sides, recent excavations have brought to light the remains of some **Iron Age huts** (13) with burial grounds. The elliptical bases of the huts can be glimpsed today where they were cut into the tuff (volcanic stone) with holes for the posts that supported walls made of reeds and mud and roofs of straw.

Just north of the "Romulean huts" you will see a rise surmounted by a grove of holm-oaks. These are the remains of the **Temple of Magna Mater** (15), the tall podium of an imposing temple dedicated to the religion of this Oriental goddess, identified with Cybele and venerated in the aniconic form of a black stone (perhaps part of a meteorite). This religion was brought to Rome in 204 BC during the second Punic war, at a time when the traditional gods of the Roman pantheon seemed to have abandoned the

city to its fate. The temple was completed only in 191 BC. Some years before this the *Ludi Megalenses* began to be held on the platform opposite: these were religious games, during which theatrical performances were also presented. The shrine has been reliably identified, partly through the discovery in the vicinity, of the cult statue of the goddess, today in the Palatine Museum.

Close by this building, as we learn from ancient sources, there were also other sanctuaries, testifying to the sacred character of the hill. Parts of them have been uncovered and identified in the most recent excavations, such as the podium of the Temple of Victory. Various items were found in its *favissae* (sacred pits), including two splendid pottery heads of divinities dated to the early 3rd century BC. They probably formed part of the decoration of the front of the temple and are in the museum. Part of the architectural decoration of another small sacred building must have been the antefixes, decorated with the head of Juno Sospita, also found in the area and dated as early as the beginning of the 5th century BC.

Podium of the Temple of the Magna Mater.

Statue of Magna Mater enthroned. Palatine Museum, Rome.

Antefixes with head of Juno Sospita, excavated on the site of the Temple of Magna Mater. Palatine Museum, Rome.

The Domus Flavia and Domus Augustana

In spite of its two names, this was actually a single, enormous residential complex, which eventually covered the whole central part of the Palatine in the late 1st century AD, obliterating the late republican buildings and part of the residence built on the hill by Nero. The building can be subdivided into

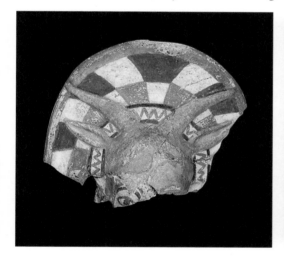

two areas: to the west the Domus Flavia, which housed the state chambers, and to the east the Domus Augustana, the private quarters of the emperor and his family. Both parts were built by the last of the Flavian emperors, Domitian, who devoted himself to the work and the innovative design by his architect Rabirius throughout his reign.

Despite the impressive brick structures that remain, what we see today is only a pale shadow of what the imperial palace must have been in ancient times: imposing chambers faced with polychrome marble, spacious colonnaded courtyards with enchanting gardens enlivened by sparkling fountains, rooms decorated with frescoes and crammed with all luxuries; and everywhere splendid statues of deities, heroes and emperors. All this has been swept away by the destructive excavations of past centuries, leaving only faint traces after the depredations. Coming from the "Augustean" zone of the hill you reach the west side of the Domus Flavia (28). This part, as can be seen by the bases of some columns, was flanked by a colonnaded portico that continued along the north side, the façade, where the main entrance to the palace was set for those coming from the Forum. The core of this area was an immense peristyle, with a large octagonal fountain in the middle. Around it were ranged all the state rooms of the Domus Flavia.

In the middle of the north side there is an enormous hall, known as the **Royal Hall**, whose walls were originally faced with marble and lined with niches containing colossal statues. In the apse at the far end of the hall was the throne of the emperor, who appeared aloof from everyone else, as dominus et deus (lord and god). This hall must have been used for official audiences and the crowded gatherings at which the whole court and many subjects came to honour the emperor. Another apsed room was set immediately to the west of this: it is described as a **basilica** because originally it was divided into a nave and side aisles by two rows of columns, like the basilicas in the Forum. A more private place, it may have been used for meetings

Reconstruction of cross-section of the Domus Flavia with the Royal Hall, the basilica and the so-called *lararium* (F. Dutert, 1845–1905). École Nationale Supérieure des Beaux-Arts, Paris.

Domus Flavia, octagonal fountain of the upper peristyle.

of the emperor's council, now that the Senate had merely formal powers. On the south side of the peristyle there was another imposing hall. It had a double floor, where warm air circulated in the cavity to heat the chamber, just one detail of the luxury in a room that the sources also describe as spectacular. This was the emperor's dining room, known as the coenatio Iovis, where the guests ate reclining on their *triclinia* (couches), with two fountains playing at the sides of the room.

Below the triclinium of Domitian some chambers have been excavated belonging to an earlier building, which the Flavian palace covered. The refinement of the frescoes on the walls and the different kinds of coloured marble laid in the floor show these were the remains of Nero's first palace, destroyed in the fire of 64 AD and replaced by the unfinished Domus Aurea.

The second area of the imperial palace, known as the Domus Augustana (29), was laid out immediately to the east of the previous complex and was set on two levels. The upper level, closely linked to the Domus Flavia, was arranged around another spacious peristyle, with a pond in the middle to which—as on a island—was erected a temple perhaps dedicated to Minerva, a goddess to whom Domitian was devoted. Most probably this peristyle also served as a viridarium (garden), where the rooms were ranged in an alternation of open and closed spaces. Unfortunately we can say little about the function of these rooms, some of which were badly damaged by the 18th-century excavations.

Domus Transitoria, vault decorated with fresco and gilded plaster.

Domus Transitoria, detail of the decoration painted with a frieze of the Battle of the Amazons.

Fragments of panels with
marble inlay that lined
the walls of the Domus
Transitoria. Palatine Museum,
Rome.

The lower levels of the complex are at present closed to the public but can be viewed from above. They face onto the Circus Maximus with a highly scenic colonnaded exedra. The rooms are not particularly large and again open onto a central courtyard, suggesting these were the living quarters of the palace. The courtyard originally had two arcaded levels, their walls probably faced with marble, which was plundered over the years. The fountain in the centre is decorated with four peltas, the typical moon-shaped shields of the Amazons.

An integral part of the imperial palace, at the eastern end of the hill, was the **Stadium** (30). This was a building of an elongated shape, with in the middle of the long eastern side a large semi-circular stand for the emperor and his family. In spite of the name, it must actually have been a large garden, also used as a riding track, a peaceful place where the emperor could stroll or be carried in a litter between beds of flowers and works of art. From this area come most of the sculptures preserved today in the Palatine Museum.

Domus Augustana, view from above of the lower peristyle and the central fountain.

Domus Augustana, view of the Stadium.

The South Corner: The Severian Buildings

To reach this zone, the visitor should go round the Stadium, passing behind the imperial platform, to a large artificial terrace that was built by Septimius Severus to enable the palace to be extended into a zone that was originally sloping. Here must have been the imperial platform from which the emperor watched the games in the circus below.

Between this platform and the Stadium were laid out the palace baths (36), an indispensable part of such an important complex. They were first built under Domitian, who supplied the water by diverting a branch of the Aqua Claudia, but entirely rebuilt by Septimius Severus.

The same emperor embellished the south corner of the hill along the Via Appia with a monumental nymphaeum-façade with a number of colonnaded floors called the Septizodium (38), of which only the foundations remain today, because it was demolished in the 16th century by Pope Sixtus V.

Portrait of a young princess found in the Palatine Stadium. Palatine Museum, Rome.

Domus Augustana, emperor's stand in the Stadium.

Arches of the substructure of the Severian area of the imperial palace (35).

The East Corner

Retracing our steps, we will end this visit to the first of the hills of Rome by leaving the enclosed area of the excavations, outside which stands the church of San Bonaventura (46), built in the Barberini vineyard, and further on, towards the Forum, the church of San Sebastiano (45). The second of these two churches is set in the middle of a spacious artificial terrace, where recent excavations have made it possible to reconstruct the architectural order: an immense arcade contained a green area, at the centre of which once stood the Temple of Elagabalus (43), last but one of the Severian emperors, who brought here all the objects most sacred to the Romans. The temple was dedicated to the Sun and the emperor, who sought to identify himself with it in an attempt to introduce at Rome the cult of the living sovereign.

View of the Circus Maximus and the southern slopes of the Palatine. Model of ancient Rome. Museo della Civiltà Romana, Rome.

The Circus Maximus

Unfortunately, because of the state of excavations and the considerable depth at which the remains are buried, all that can be seen is a small part of the stairs on the side of the south curve: little enough if we remember that the Circus Maximus is one of the biggest buildings for entertainments that has ever existed.

In ancient times it took the form of a structure set on a rectangular plan with curves at two shorter sides. It was surrounded by steps carried on several rows of arches which could seat over 200,000 people. Running down the middle was a longitudinal structure—the *spina*—around which the chariots raced. Set on the *spina*, as we know from images in mosaics, were two obelisks brought from Egypt, some small shrines and aedicules, and seven eggs and dolphins in bronze that served to count the laps.

According to tradition, the first wooden stadium used for races, set in the valley between the Palatine and Aventine, was built by Tarquinius Priscus. Without doubt, however, the present building is the result of centuries of extensions and rebuilding. First the timber structures were replaced by stone steps, then in the late 4th century BC the *carceres*, the starting bays for the horses, were built at the short north end. Under Augustus the first obelisk, that of Rameses II, was erected on the *spina* (it is now in Piazza del Popolo). After this period the stadium was damaged by various fires: after the one in 64 AD, Nero had it almost completely rebuilt and increased its seating capacity, while the damage caused by a fire under Domitian was rapidly made good by Trajan, to whom we largely owe the structure now visible.

The Circus Maximus was one of the most crowded places in Rome, at least until the 4th century AD, when chariot races, with the most important being held during the *Ludi Romani*, were at the height of their popularity, to the point where in this period the four chariot teams (*factiones*), who were distinguished by colour, actually developed into political groupings. The last games were organised in 549 AD. After this, largely because of the dereliction of Rome in the early Middle Ages, it gradually began to be covered in soil, which today conceals most of the building. (*M.C.G.*)

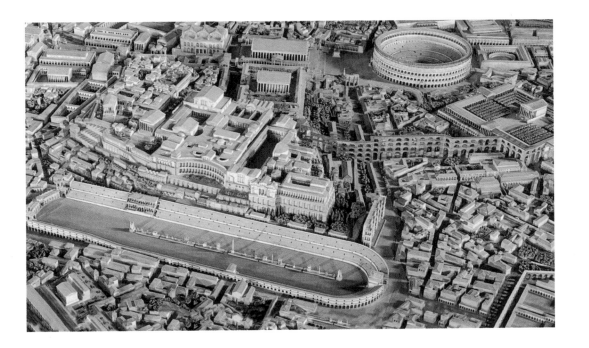

The Farnese Gardens
and Picnics on the Grand Tour

The Farnese Gardens today.

The Farnese Gardens
in a painting by A.L.R. Ducros
(1748–1810). Musée Cantonal
des Beaux-Arts, Lausanne.

To add lustre to his family and as a sign of its power, in the 16th century Cardinal Alessandro Farnese, grandson of Paul III, laid out the Farnese Gardens on the ancient remains of the Palatine, a richly symbolic site in the history of Rome. The villa, surrounded by luxuriant gardens for the pleasure of the family and as a venue for magnificent receptions, is said to have been planned by Michelangelo himself, but should perhaps be attributed to Vignola and Rainaldi. This appears in the style of the imposing portal that once formed the main entrance to the gardens, facing the Forum, and has now been reassembled as a monumental gateway to the archaeological area on Via di San Gregorio. The gardens were laid out on a series of terraces linked by flights of steps that rose past the nymphaeum, called the Ninfeo della Pioggia, and culminated in the Teatro del Fontanone. Its centre lay in the frescoed Casina, surmounted by aviaries filled with brilliantly plumed exotic birds that created a synaesthesia of sounds and colours. A system of underground passages for "al fresco" walks was laid out in the base of the Domus Tiberiana, which also provided the substructure for gardens in the Italian style, decorated with ancient

sculptures found in those same years on the Palatine, used for the meetings of Arcadia and arousing the wonder of visitors. When ownership passed to the Bourbon kings of Naples, what had become the first botanical and zoological garden in the world fell into decay until in the 18th and 19th centuries travellers on the Grand Tour rediscovered the romantic beauty of the hill, immersed in a luxuriant landscape with majestic ruins. Here the tourists enjoyed, as we still can today, an incomparable panorama of the city. Curiously excavations of ancient and modern strata have turned up fragments of English tableware used on outings and afternoon picnics and left on the hillside, clear traces of these "noble" visitors. (*N.G.*)

Apollo in the House of Augustus: Living with the God

Detail of the statue of Augustus as *pontifex maximus*, from the Via Labicana, late 1st century BC. Museo Nazionale Romano, Palazzo Massimo alle Terme, Rome.

One of three feminine herms of the Danaides in black ancient marble that decorated, according to the sources, the portico of the Temple of Apollo. Palatine Museum, Rome.

Terracotta plaque of Apollo and Heracles (i.e. Octavian and Mark Anthony) contending for the Delphic tripod. Palatine Museum, Rome.

Detail of the "Campanian" plaque of Athens and Perseus with the Gorgon. The exhibit in the Palatine Museum retains part of the lively polychrome decoration.

The character and the appearance of the Palatine underwent a radical change in the reign of Augustus. When he was still only Octavian, he was born and lived on the other side of the hill: subsequently he established his residence on the site of *Roma Quadrata* (the earliest inhabited nucleus) near the "hut of Romulus" and stairs of Cacus, not far from the Temple of Cybele (whose legend confirmed the Trojan origins of the city) and the Temple of Victory, in allusion to his military triumphs. To do this the *princeps* had to buy and restore a number of houses, some of which belonged to important figures in the literary and political life of the time. To make the hill even more sacred he organised a solemn inauguration, sung by the court poets, of the Temple of Apollo (21), erected in 28 BC in a part of the house that had been struck by lightning, which the soothsayers declared had been chosen by the god. This temple was his *ex voto* for the victory over Mark Antony after the naval battle of Actium in 31 BC. The bare concrete nucleus of the podium, which today is all we see, fails to evoke the original splendour of the building. Built entirely in white Luni marble (from present-day Massa Carrara), its doors were made of gold and ivory. Archaic statues in Parian marble decorated the pediment while the cult images were works by the greatest sculptors of the 4th century BC. These statues were specially brought from Greece and set up inside the cell, which overflowed with treasures: the ancient authors attribute to Cephisodotus the figure of Latona, to Timotheus that of Diana, while the image of Apollo is a masterpiece of Skopas, of which some fragments, per-

haps, of the face and foot, are now in the Palatine Museum. In the base of the statue of Apollo, Augustus placed the Sibylline books, containing prophecies of the future of Rome and the Empire, which had previously been preserved in the Temple of Capitoline Jupiter.

The shrine was distinguished from all other Roman temples by being closely integrated with the residence of the emperor and by the staginess of its typically Hellenistic design. The complex, laid out on two terraces linked by steps dominating the Circus Maximus, did, in fact, actually include hanging gardens and a square set in front of it, where four bases supported the famous bronze cows by Myron (5th century BC), surrounded by a portico of columns in *giallo antico* decorated with the statues of the fifty mythical daughters of Danaus: at the instigation of their father, they are said to have murdered their Egyptian husbands on the day of their marriage, and were punished in Hades by being perpetually forced to carry water in pots full of holes. Some of these figures have been recovered in excavations of the site, together with numerous slabs of polychrome terracotta of very high quality representing sacred and mythical subjects related to the cult of Apollo. Augustus sought to identify himself with this god, who was the defender of morality and order, moderation and peace, as a propaganda move to win support for his difficult transition from Republic to Empire.

To strengthen the consensus surrounding an ideology that, while seeming to preserve of the traditional political, moral and cultural values, actually undermined them, Augustus showed great insight in relying on the power of images and symbols, choosing a figurative language marked with an eclectic classicism.

We have already seen that, as at Pergamum and Alexandria, the shrine was closely integrated with the private residence of the sovereign, being set in the wing that contained the state rooms, a series of spacious chambers laid out round a peristyle, with precious marble paving, walls faced with equally splendid materials, and refined stucco ceilings. The emperor's private quarters were much plainer and more Spartan (20), separated by a road paved with freestone from those of his wife Livia (19). Various rooms, lined with simpler mosaics of black tiles with white crosses, still preserve a fresco cycle of extraordinary freshness in what is called the "Style

Fragment of plaster painted with Apollo Citharedeus, from the area of the House of Augustus. Palatine Museum, Rome.

House of Augustus, Room of the Masks, west wall with backdrop alluding to the satyr plays.

House of Augustus, detail of the refined painted decoration of the "studiolo."

On pages 82–83
House of Augustus, Room of the Pine Festoons.

II advanced." The Room of the Masks, so called from a series of masked figures, both young and old, portrayed with great vivacity ranged along the cornice. This decoration is important for the study of ancient perspective, with its different points of view and skilful use of shading. The walls recreate the illusion of a real wooden stage set placed against the stone wall, enlivened with recesses and ledges, while the stage doors have curtains decorated with rural landscapes to suit the plays represented on different occasions. To the same period also belongs the **Room of the Pine Festoons**, which has a decorative pattern common in the houses in Pompeii: realistic pine branches set between narrow wooden pillars arranged on a high podium in front of a wall where, beyond them at the top, a portico can also be seen. But the chamber that surpasses all others for refinement and variety of pictorial motives is definitely the upper *cubiculum* or bed-chamber (also called the "**studiolo**"), recomposed after long and painstaking restoration. Beneath a ceiling in which stucco panels alternate with traditional paintings, with red, yellow and black grounds and pure white architectural elements overgrown with the vegetation, there are certain details drawn with striking mastery: swans, chalices, winged gryphons and lotus flowers reveal the Alexandrian origins of a great artist who must have come to Rome in the retinue of the victor of Actium. It was here, to his "Syracuse," that Augustus would withdraw when he wished to remain undisturbed; here he concealed from everyone's eyes his secret Hellenistic "modernity" tinged with a certain Nilotic exoticism; here he could meditate as he gazed from the window at the Temple of Apollo, his patron deity. In this "workshop" he would also dabble in carpentry or read the books in the two symmetrical libraries in the east sector of the house that can be recognised in the rebuilding of the Flavian period. This also helps explain the name of Domus Augustana preserved by Domitian's palace—inevitably the subsequent emperors erected their residences next to that of their venerated predecessor—and the excessively small dimensions of the excavated part of the House of Augustus. (*N.G.*)

The House of Livia: An "Annex" for the Empress

The discovery of lead piping bearing the inscription Iulia Augusta proves that Livia lived in the two-story house dating from the late republican period (75–50 BC), set in the tuff (volcanic stone) of the hillside (19) to the north of that of her husband Augustus (20). Perhaps it was there that she gave birth to Tiberius, the son of her first husband and the future emperor. Naturally this was before the interior of the Augustean complex became the emperor's private apartments, refurbished and embellished with decorations (30–20 BC) worthy of its new status. By going down the steps and through a sloping passage, today you can enter an atrium that must have been covered by a roof borne on two pillars and with a floor, like the whole house, paved with a simple mosaic. This little courtyard was an island of coolness flanked by a small dining room (*triclinium*) on the south-west and a small reception room (*tablinum*), flanked by two rooms (*alae*) to the southeast. The panels with their pictorial decoration in the "Style II advanced," which have made this residence famous, have been replaced on the walls of the rooms. On entering the **tablinum** the visitor finds imaginary doors opening on three sides and framing familiar mythological scenes based on famous Greek paintings: Mercury freeing Io, loved by Jupiter, from impri-

Portrait of Livia, found
in the bed of the Tiber,
late 1st century BC. Museo
Nazionale Romano, Palazzo
Massimo alle Terme, Rome.

A realistic-looking mosaic
doormat at the rear entrance
to the House of Livia.

House of Livia, frescos
on a wall of the *tablinum*
with a genre scene from
the Hellenistic repertory
in a panel set on a frame
of the backdrop.

House of Livia, left wing, the
Room of the Winged Figures.

sonment by Argus, a hundred-eyed giant, to whom Juno had given her out of jealousy for "safe-keeping," Galataea on a sea horse fleeing from Polyphemus against the backdrop of Mt. Aetna, etc. The various architectural elements that frame the scenes create multiple perspectives and complex planes of reality that enchant the eye, while the gaze is attracted by the motives in Egyptian style of the friezes and *acroteria* (pedestals for statues, etc.). Finally, there are highly original views opening onto city streets with lively scenes, with houses and figures appearing at their windows. In the **left wing** the main interest of the decoration lies in the panels on the upper level. Here pairs of fantastic figures (Gryphons, Winged Victories), are set heraldically beside candlesticks and perched on the branches of the tree of life, rendered in colours that fade into the white ground: these are the "eccentricities" that Vitruvius condemned in the same period. In the **right wing**, the side walls are decorated with an elegant portico of Corinthian columns with luxuriant festoons of leaves, flowers and fruits, tied with multi-coloured ribbons from which hang objects associated with rural cults. The decoration, similar to that carved on the inner enclosure of the Ara Pacis, evokes the mythical Age of Gold renewed under the Augustan principate. At the top, sequences of figures, animals, places of worship, ritual scenes, represented impressionistically, make this yellow frieze one of the most significant examples of Roman landscape painting. But the palace did not end here: a staircase led to an upper level of which there remain some chambers and service rooms visible on the outside, like the original atrium with the east door, later walled up to adapt it to the Domus Augustea. At home Livia retained her influence and independence and defended herself from Augustus's scandalous partiality for young women, whom he enjoyed deflowering and who were supplied in large numbers—as the gossipy but well-informed Suetonius records—by his Livia herself, now getting on in years. (*N.G.*)

Under the Sign of Isis

Not far from the Casa dei Grifi, today cut through by the massive foundations of the basilica of the Palace of Domitian, there used to stand a spacious and luxurious late republican *domus,* of which all that remains is a large rectangular chamber with an apse set in the shorter side. Here were discovered the remains of some highly interesting Style II advanced paintings. The walls were detached to prevent further decay: watercolours and drawings had been made as soon as it was discovered and fortunately document mythological or ritual scenes now lost. Recently restored, they are now exhibited in a room of the Domus Augustana in the Loggia Mattei. The decorations of this chamber, which is called the **Aula Isiaca** (32) because of the numerous decorative motives related to the religion of Isis (the *situla* or drinking vessel, wreathed roses in the snood, lotus flower, solar disk, the snake from the crushed body, etc.), were first dated to the age of Caligula, because of the emperor's devotion to the ancient Egyptian goddess. Careful critical revision, however, related the cycle to the period of Augustus, when, after his victory at Actium, Isidian and Egyptian motives became fashionable in Rome and, freed from any religious significance, were used purely for the sake of ornament. Finally some scholars believe this was the House of Mark Antony on the Palatine, which passed after his death to Agrippa. Agrippa may well also have been the owner of the Villa of the Farnesina, whose splendid paintings (now in Palazzo Massimo alle Terme) can be attributed to artists who had much in common with those that decorated the Aula Isiaca. (*N.G.*)

Aula Isiaca, detail of the pictorial decoration with Isidian and Egyptian motives. Though classical white grounds dominate, heightening the chromatic contrasts, in the vault the artist abandoned the traditional subjects presented on the walls, indulging in an expressive freedom rare in ancient decoration. This can be clearly seen in the red ribbon interwoven with a sinuous band of blue, framed by lotus flowers and large yet delicate rose petals with curled edges. It is a kaleidoscope of bright hues (blue, green, violet, yellow, pink), rendered even more brilliant by the rich gold highlights.

The Loggia Mattei:
The Renaissance on the Palatine

The Loggia Mattei
before restoration.

Loggia Mattei, detail
of frieze with masks.

Loggia Mattei, general view
of the vault after restoration.

The Palatine was transformed over the centuries into a select district where important families like the Farnese established their residences. It was the Farnese that—as we saw—created the stage-like perspective of the gardens that recede from the hill towards the valley with the Forum. On the hilltop another small villa had already been erected between the Domus Flavia and the Stadium in the 14th century: the small villa of the Stati, which was acquired in the 16th century by the Mattei family and then enlarged and embellished with the creation of a striking pattern of avenues planted with laurel, myrtle, and cypresses. On these structures was laid out the neo-Gothic Villa Mills, demolished together with other buildings when systematic excavations were undertaken with the sole aim of bringing to light the imperial ruins. However, respect for its rich fresco decorations ensured the preservation of a Renaissance loggia, today set within a Roman hall on a rectangular plan and re-roofed in modern times. The Loggia consists of a row of three columns with ancient shafts of grey granite, surmounted with Ionic capitals in travertine dating from the 16th century, with egg motives moulded in stucco and with traces of gilding. The columns support round-headed arches. The vault is frescoed with "grotesque" patterns and divided up geometrically by elegant cornices and friezes with masks, enlivened with festoons of laurel framing the panels which represent mythological scenes. On

90

the corbels there are aedicules painted with six of the Muses, Apollo and Athene. In the spandrels are tondi with the signs of the zodiac, while the lunettes on the walls present scenes from the story of Venus. The Loggia was built by the Mattei family, who merely had it restored and enlarged, as shown by the coat of arms in the middle of the vault. In the 1520s, the Stati commissioned Baldassarre Peruzzi to devise the decorative scheme and he, as was customary, employed a team of assistants to paint the decorations. The paintings of mythological scenes and signs of the zodiac, which found a ready sale on the antiquarian market, were unfortunately removed from their ornamental context, transferred to canvas and removed elsewhere in the mid-19th century. In the course of the recent restoration, a generous long-term loan of the scenes, today the property of the Metropolitan Museum of Art, has made it possible to completely recompose the pictorial decoration of the vault, the only surviving example of Renaissance painting on the Palatine. (*N.G.*)

The Casa dei Grifi:
A Spectacle for Many
but Not for All

Many of the visitors that climb to the top of the Palatine to admire the ruins of the Domus Flavia set in an idyllic landscape are unaware that these buildings by Nero and Domitian covered the most interesting republican residence of Rome. It clearly belonged to a member of the aristocracy, given the refinement of its decorative scheme (31). The building was laid out on two floors that were adapted to the original slope of the hill and with various chambers arranged around the atrium. It was built in the 2nd century BC, as is shown by the building technique employed (*opus incertum* with some rebuilding using a technique close to *opus reticulatum*). In about 120–100 BC it was covered with an important fresco cycle and laid with rich mosaic floors. Two large Gryphons in heraldic pose, fashioned in white

Casa dei Grifi, lunette
with Gryphons in stucco, today
only partly preserved.

Casa dei Grifi, view
of the interior showing location
of the rooms.

Casa dei Grifi, a perfectly
preserved corner reveals
the vivid original colouring
of the paintings.

stucco, face a luxuriant acanthus plant that stands out against the red plaster ground of a lunette. The Gryphons have given their name to the house,
which is again accessible, after lengthy restoration, but only to small groups
with advance bookings for the sake of conservation. You then pass through
an anonymous gate leading to a lawn and then, by a steep slight of steps, you
enter a series of dimly evocative interiors where soft, specially designed
lighting enables you to admire the brilliant colours, elsewhere lost. Whole
rooms and fragments of wall are covered with the most ancient Style II
paintings that have come down to us. Here is the first illusionistic representation of columns, set on bases decorated with lozenges on a dark ground
that seem to project from the wall. However there is still no attempt to open
out the wall into backdrops painted in perspective—as we found in the later
examples in the House of Livia—but the artists have rendered in paint the
structure of a wall built out of blocks of stone, which the earlier system of
decoration imitated in relief, with stucco encrustations. The orthostates,
pilasters, dressed stonework, cornices and friezes seem to be made out of
the most attractive and precious marble of the ancient world: alabaster,
onyx, *cipollino* marble, porphyry, breccia, *rosso antico* and *giallo antico*.
Though using exclusively architectural motives, the painting recreates the
illusion of an elegant interior, enhanced by the black and white mosaic floors bounded by a coloured band running round the perimeter. In the centre
of one room is the most ancient example in Rome of a *scutulatum*, a square
with a pattern of cubes in perspective (repeating the pattern of the continuous podium on the walls), laid in polychrome stones and marbles of inexpressible fascination and modernity. While the richest stores of ancient
painting have been found in Pompeii and Herculaneum, whose remains
historically laid the basis for the division into decorative styles, the Casa dei
Grifi, like the other frescoed houses on the Palatine, reveal—as might have
been predicted—that the models for their art were created by the imperial
dynasty and the Roman aristocracy before spreading rapidly outwards.
(*N.G.*)

Casa dei Grifi, wall with
refined Style II architectural
decoration, showing the
elegant cornice and the use
of pastel hues.

Casa dei Grifi, the great
cubiculum with its walls wholly
preserved. This decoration,
more advanced than earlier
schemes, consists of three
planes with different depths.
The room's fresco decorations,
previously removed for
preservation and displayed
in the museum, were returned
to their original position
during the recent restoration.

Casa dei Grifi, the *scutulatum emblem* in the middle of the mosaic floor of the *cubiculum*.

The Palatine Museum: From the Origins of Rome to Imperial Splendour

Palatine Museum, view of Room V containing material of the Augustan period.
In the foreground a statue of Hermes with head of a Julian-Claudian prince (?); in the niche the surviving fragments of the cult statue of the Palatine Apollo carved by Skopas; under the bracket a Corinthian capital of exquisite workmanship. On the wall nearby the display cases with the elegant "Campanian" earthenware polychrome plaques.

Founded in the later 19th century as an Antiquarium to preserve art works discovered in the excavations of the hill, the Palatine Museum has occupied different buildings in its chequered history. Only recently, as part of the general reorganization of Rome's museums, the City's Archaeological Service has decided to make full use of the premises of the convent of the nuns of the Visitation built in 1868 over that part of the Domus Flavia that was joined to the Domus Augustana. The skilfully designed display presents, on two levels, both the exhibition of works from the latest archaeological studies of early phases of settlement on the hill and of the Romulean city, as well as the illustration of the refined artistic culture of the imperial palaces from the age of Augustus to the late empire.

The visit begins on the **ground floor** with rooms that contain parts of the original structures that have been obliterated: for example the remains of one of the two elliptical nymphaeums built at the sides of the sumptuous triclinium of the Domus Flavia and the corner of a bath from the Neronian period, which comes from the sector of the Domus Aurea on the Palatine. The first rooms (I–III) contain the archaeological documentation of prehistory (from the Palaeolithic to the Bronze Age) and the early historical period (10th–7th century BC) of settlement on the hill. Models reconstruct the human presence on the Palatine in the Iron Age, with huts and sepulchres. In Room IV the sacred and religious significance of the hill is explored in the archaic and republican periods (6th–1st centuries BC), with exhibition of the finds from the cult centres (the temples of the Magna Mater and the Temple of Victory) or from private houses. Some architectural fragments also reveal that in the same period the Palatine had become the favoured residential area for the Roman ruling class.

On the **upper floor**, the great hall of Room V presents the symbols of the ideological propaganda of Augustus (54–68 AD, the first emperor, who radically altered the appearance of the Palatine, as was also done later by Nero (54–68 AD) (Room VI). It is impossible to record here all the exhibits (statues, carved marble slabs, marble intarsia, frescos detached from their original locations, altars, the busts of philosophers and the portraits of emperors) which are on display in Rooms VII–VIII and in the Gallery (Room IX), which document the magnificent pictorial and sculptural decorations (Greek originals and Roman copies) that once embellished the imperial residences, from the Julian-Claudian age to the Tetrarchy (4th century AD). We have chosen to illustrate the most significant works within the context of their provenances. (*N.G.*)

The Capitol
and the Capitoline
Museums

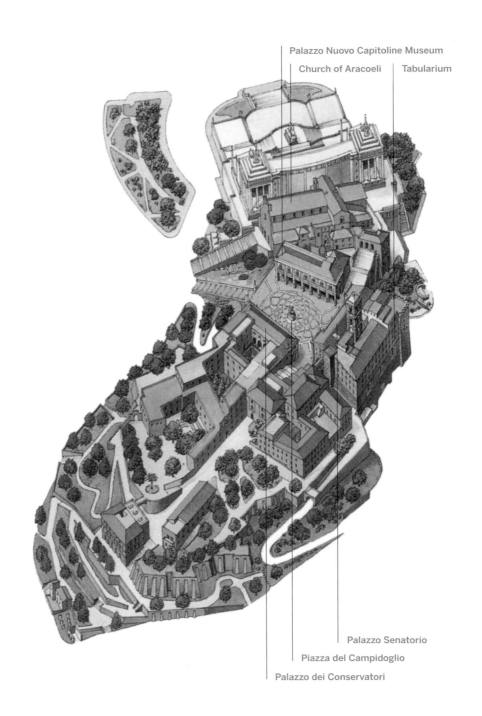

Palazzo Nuovo Capitoline Museum

Church of Aracoeli   Tabularium

Palazzo Senatorio

Piazza del Campidoglio

Palazzo dei Conservatori

Suggestions for a Visit

The Capitol is a museum complex
of extraordinary historical and cultural
significance: it is a single, organic complex
made up of the square, the palaces, the
archaeological and historical-artistic
collections, plus now, with the reopening
of the underground entrance, also the
major ancient monuments. Then there
is the inexpressible fascination of the views
over pagan and Christian Rome; and an
even more theatrical and scenic
atmosphere at night. That perfection,
that sense of magical harmony, that you
breathe as you climb up to the Capitol
by the monumental flight of steps, is not
just the result of Michelangelo's refined
architectural design. The layout of the
square, though surrounded by buildings,
opens like a stage towards the city and
is above all the creation of the millennia
of history that have treated the hill of the
Capitol hill as the religious and political
heart of Rome. The route of this visit to the
Capitoline Museums, with some of the
most significant historical and artistic
works selected for comment, begins at the
Palazzo Nuovo, which houses the
Capitoline Museum, on the left of the
square as you ascend the steps to the hill.

The Capitol

<u>In Antiquity.</u> The name "Capitol" once seems to have meant "dominant height," though an ancient tradition derives it from a skull (*caput*) found when the foundations were being dug for the Temple of Capitoline Jupiter. Originally the hill consisted of two wooded heights, the Arx and the Capitolium, separated by a small valley that contained the Asylum, the area Romulus is said to have thrown open to the inhabitants of nearby towns to swell the population of the growing city. Recent archaeological finds have, in fact, illuminated the truth of the legends handed down about the origins of Rome and the myth of its foundation. Near Palazzo dei Conservatori traces have emerged of even earlier settlement of the hills in the late Bronze Age (1200–1000 BC).

Evidence of this has been found in children's graves as well as the remains of metalworking. It was the last of the kings of Rome who was responsible for the definitive consecration of the Capitolium. The Tarquins built the Temple of Jupiter Optimus Maximus, dedicated to the Capitoline Triad (Jupiter, Juno, Minerva) venerated in three cells of the building. Of the temple, noted in the sources for its lavish decorations, the strong foundations are still perfectly preserved and were incorporated into the substructure of the Renaissance Palazzo Caffarelli. The temple, inaugurated in the first year of the Republican period (509 BC), became the symbol of Roman civilisation. It was duplicated in all the new cities founded by Rome and all triumphal processions culminated here. It was customary for the victorious generals, on returning from conquest, to march in procession through the city with their retinue of prisoners and booty of war along the Via Sacra to the Capitolium where they performed sacrifices. The other height on the Capitol, strongly fortified and with steep, rugged slopes, was the Acropolis (Arx) of the city. Where the arresting volume of the Church of Aracoeli now rises, there formerly stood the Temple of Juno Moneta, which, because of the security of its location, housed the public mint.

By 78 BC the slopes of the Capitol towards the Forum had been smoothed by the construction of the majestic structures of the Tabularium, the public archives in which the Roman State preserved thousands of documents and the texts of laws. When the building was erected, care was taken to respect the small, existing (196 BC) sanctuary of Veiovis (adolescent Jove), a mysterious Italic deity who was close to the world of Hades and the patron god of outcasts, highly popular during the Republic. In this

Under a Pile of Shields

A sad legend surrounds the heroine who gave her name to the cliff on the Capitol, where criminals were hurled to their deaths. (Its exact location is now uncertain because of subsidence of the valley walls.) She was the daughter of Tarpieus, whom Romulus left in charge of the Capitoline fortress when he left to make war on the Sabines. The girl fell in love with the Sabine king Titus Tatius, encamped with his army on the slope of the hill, and she made a terrible pact with him: if he married her, she would open the gates of the citadel to his army. Her hopes were short-lived. After entering the fortress, her treacherous suitor ordered his soldiers to crush her under the weight of their shields. However, another version of the legend has it that Tarpeia only pretended to betray her people with the intent of disarming the enemy, asking each Sabine for his shield as identification. On discovering the plot, her rash lover took a dreadful revenge. (*N.G.*)

period the square surrounding the Temple of Jupiter (Area Capitolina) was enriched with numerous monuments (small temples, altars, porticos, statues, arches, etc.) commissioned from the greatest artists of the time by the leading families of the Roman nobility as propaganda.

From the Middles Ages to the Renaissance

In the Middles Ages the buildings fell into ruin or were knocked down to scavenge materials; the marble stripped from them was cast into furnaces to make lime. An echo of the ancient grandeur—already tarnished by spoliation and calamity but also by the last emperors, who despoiled Rome to embellish Constantinople—can be heard in the descriptions of the *Mirabilia Urbis* ("Wonders of Rome"). While the ruins of the Temple of Jupiter had become, by an irony of fate, a goat pasture (Monte Caprino), the still massive remains of the Tabularium were fortified in the 11th century by powerful baronial families engaged in the struggle for supremacy. Then in 1143, the citizens of Rome declared the city a self-governing Commune, and authority was vested, after an anti-papal revolution, in senators installed in the palace that takes its name from them. The marble facing of the Renaissance façade in fact conceals the fortified and battlemented towers (from the 14th and 15th centuries) that are visible at the sides, strengthening the corners of a fortress that stood at the centre of the city's life, though now it is rather on the edge of the inner city. The Palazzo Senatorio, which is still Rome's city hall, possessed a tower (damaged and rebuilt in a central position in the 16th century) to which the citizens would be summoned by the pealing of a bell called the *patarina*. This bell had been carried off in battle from Viterbo in 1200 and returned to the city only in the early 19th century. The opening of a loggia on the square

where the market was held inverted the perspective: while in the Roman period the principal monuments on the hill faced the Forum, in the Middles Ages the Capitol opened out towards the Campus Martius. In 1363, with the first city statutes, a single senator from outside the city was flanked by three elective magistrates, known as the Conservatori, who represented the new social classes who had come to power and now controlled the administration of the city. It was in this period that the buildings that existed before must have been transformed into the magnificent Palazzo dei Conservatori. It has a portico on the ground floor, while the first floor has Guelf-cross windows, and from the start it housed the collection of antiquities from the Capitol. Down to the 15th century relations between the institutions of the city and the papacy were not always peaceful. In 1471, with an astute political move, Pope Sixtus IV gave the Roman people the "famous bronze statues" till then kept in

the Lateran palace. The transfer of the sculptures, which represented the continuity between ancient Rome and the temporal power of the papacy, was intended to reassert the predominance of the Church over the municipal autonomy. This action made the Capitol the place of memory: the She-Wolf, with the figures of Romulus and Remus added, were exhibited on the façade of the Palazzo dei Conservatori and became the symbol of the city.

The Piazza: An Experiment in Perfection

In 1536, when work was being carried out to embellish the city for the arrival of the emperor Charles V, the Farnese pope Paul III commissioned Michelangelo to confer architectural unity on the rather heterogeneous set of buildings on the Capitol. Over the next two years he produced a brilliant project, dominated by the equestrian statue of Marcus Aurelius. This had to be brought specially from the Lateran and placed in the wonderful star-shaped pattern in the paving, known from engravings but only laid in 1940. (The original statue has now been replaced by a faithful copy to ensure its preservation.) Michelangelo's plans for the piazza began to be executed in the following decades, mainly by Giacomo Della Porta, and ended over a century later with the completion of the Palazzo Nuovo, on the left of the square. Its front elevation mirrors that of the Palazzo dei Conservatori and ensures the symmetry of the whole. The harmony was also enhanced by adopting for all three buildings the gigantic order, with massive cornices and balustrades embellished with statues. Also carefully calculated was the use of voids and solids, the colouring, decorations and friezes, all features that can be appreciated after the recent careful restoration of their surfaces. The project began with additions to the Palazzo Senatorio, which was given a double staircase leading to the *piano nobile*, the only work that Michelangelo saw finished. With the arrival of the Acqua Felice, a fountain was set against the staircase. It has a double superimposed basin in Greek marble flanked by two statues of river gods originally from the baths of Constantine on the Quirinal but already present on the Capitol at the time. On the left, the personification of the Nile rests one arm on a sphinx and supports the cornucopia of fertility and plenty; while in the group representing the Tiber on the right, for the glory of Rome what was originally a tiger was transformed into a she-wolf. Finally the large central niche contained an excessively small statue of Minerva seated, with drapery carved in porphyry (a prized imperial red marble) and restored as Rome Triumphant with the addition of some typical attributes of the goddess.

The façade of the Palazzo Senatorio thus formed a dramatic climax to a path that began with the gentle ascent by a balustraded flight of steps. This was enriched over the years with important sculptures: from the ancient Egyptian lions transformed into fountains at the foot of the hills to the gigantic groups of the Dioscuri recomposed at the top of the steps. The Dioscuri (Castor and Pollux) were the sons of Zeus. Legend has it they appeared in the city to announce the Roman victory over the Latins at Lake Regillus (499 or 496 BC) and watered their horses in the spring of the nymph Juturna in the Forum. (*N.G.*)

The Piazza del Campidoglio with the façade of the Palazzo dei Conservatori, after the recent restoration.

The Long History
of the Capitoline Museums

Formation and Display of the Collections. The collections of the Capitoline Museums were assembled over a span of five centuries and reflect the most significant moments in the history of Rome from the Renaissance to the modern age. The origins of the Capitoline Museums lie in the cultural setting of the 15th century, when the archaeological heritage was considered not just as a source of building materials, as had been the case through most of the Middle Ages, but as collectibles of great antiquarian interest. An inscription at the entrance to the Palazzo dei Conservatori commemorates Sixtus IV's restitution to the Roman people,

in 1471, of four ancient bronzes: the She-Wolf, a colossal head of Constantine—with the hand and the globe—the Spinarius and the so-called Gypsy Woman. These works formed the core of the first public collection of antiquities.

The pontiff's gesture marked the start of the return to the Capitol of numerous important ancient sculptures. The Conservatori themselves acquired the gilded bronze statue of Hercules which was found, also under the papacy of Sixtus IV, in the Forum Boarium near the church of Santa Maria in Cosmedin, and made it a "monument to the glory of Rome." Some years later the remains of the colossal statue of Constantine, recovered in 1486 in the basilica of Maxentius, were also brought to Palazzo dei Conservatori.

On page 110
Courtyard of Palazzo
dei Conservatori.

These works were added to the few existing on the hill in the Middle Ages, all linked closely with the symbolic function of the municipal headquarters. Among them were the marble group representing a lion attacking a horse, formerly set at the top of the staircase of Palazzo Senatorio, where death sentences were pronounced and sometimes executed. This was followed by the funerary urns from the Mausoleum of Augustus, which had been used in the Capitoline market as measures for grain and salt. In the first half of the 14th century Cola di Rienzo had collected a set of inscriptions on the Capitol, and these were the nucleus of the municipal collection. It was distinguished, at least down to the mid-16th century, for the outstanding historical value of the inscriptions, which were chosen more for historical value than their intrinsic artistic qualities. In this way, as we have seen, the addition of the twins to the She-Wolf effaced the rather sinister associations it had acquired as a symbol of justice on the Lateran and stressed its more auspicious image as the Mater Romanorum, the emblem of the city, in which it replaced the lion. The three historical reliefs from a monument erected in honour of Marcus Aurelius, from the church of Santi Luca e Martina al Foro, had already been moved in 1515 to the Palazzo dei Conservatori, where their subjects—the submission of the barbarians, the triumph and the sacrifice before the Temple of Capitoline Jupiter—were considered to represent an ideal continuity between the ancient world and the Renaissance Capitol. In 1538 Paul III transferred from the Lateran the equestrian statue of Marcus Aurelius, which had escaped the systematic melting and reuse suffered by most ancient bronzes because in the Middle Ages it was believed to represent Constantine, the first Christian emperor. In 1541 Paul III also donated a large statue of Athene, which was placed in the central niche of the staircase of Palazzo Senatorio and is now in the atrium of the Palazzo Nuovo. Michelangelo's reorganisation of Piazza del Campidoglio was followed by a reordering of the sculptures and inscriptions preserved in the palace. Thanks to the descriptions of scholars and valuable drawings by many different artists, we know with a fair degree of accuracy the arrangement of the collections from the beginning of the 16th century. Until the second half of the 16th century the various important acquisitions that followed—the Fasti Consolari, the work known as the Capitoline Brutus, the tables with the Lex de imperio Vespasiani, almost a decalogue, in the modern sense, against sin—respect the original historical nature of the collection. This continuity was interrupted in 1566 when Pius V, wishing "to purge the Vatican of pagan idols," decided to transfer to the Capitol a series of works whose purely artistic character laid the foundations for a true museum of ancient art.

In the 17th century the growth of the collection was limited because it had to compete with private collectors on the antiquarian market. All the same the overcrowding of the spaces occupied by statuary in the Palazzo dei Conservatori began to hinder the ancient municipal magistracy in the performance of their duties in these chambers, which were their place of office and representation. Already at the end of the 17th century there was an exodus of sculptures to the Palazzo Nuovo opposite, completed in 1654 by Carlo Rainaldi. But the building's function as a museum only became established in 1733 with the purchase by Clement XII of an outstanding collection of busts of illustrious men, emperors and philosophers that had belonged to Cardinal Albani. He paid for it out of the revenue from the game of lotto organised in the square of the Capitol. After the museum was inaugurated in 1734, with a plan for the protection and development of the artistic and archaeological heritage of the Papal State, further donations were made by Clement XII and of Benedict XIV. Masterpieces like the erroneously named Dying Gladiator, the Venus Capitolina and the group of Amor and Psyche enriched the museum. Along the staircase were arranged the fragments of the *Forma Urbis Romae* (a marble plan of the city from the Severian period, discovered in the 16th century in near the Forum Pacis), where it remained down to the beginning of the last century. Among the most important acquisitions in the later 18th century were two Centaurs now set in the middle of the great hall and the very fine mosaic of the Doves: all had been found, like the Faun in *rosso antico* marble, in the villa of the emperor Hadrian I at Tivoli and given by Clement XIII.

The installation in Palazzo Nuovo of this extraordinary collection of ancient sculptures renders the Capitoline Museum an interesting example of 18th-century principles of museum design, which favoured an arrangement by categories, with the position of the individual works dictated on refined aesthetic principles. They have remained essentially unchanged for over 250 years, as we find by comparison with drawings from the 18th and 19th centuries. Even the way works were restored, with the reconstruction and reinterpretation of ancient sculptures, is a fundamental document of the cultivated taste of collectors in past centuries.

The foundation of the Museo Pio Clementino in the Vatican in 1771 was a setback for new archaeological endowments: the concern of the popes from that time on was to expand their new museum.

The French Revolution and Napoleonic wars affected the Capitol, which saw some of its masterpieces taken to France and only in part recovered after the fall of Napoleon by the tenacity of Canova, at that time the museum's director. In 1838 the Capitoline Museum was returned to the Conservatori; in exchange the museum had to give up its rich assortment of Egyptian antiquities, which were moved to the Vatican. The Castellani donations (mostly Greek and Etruscan-Italic vases, including the famous cratera of Aristonothos), together with the creation of the museum's collection of medals, were the major events on the eve of the proclamation of Rome as capital of a united Italy (1870).

Stefano della Bella, courtyard of Palazzo dei Conservatori in the 16th century.

The feverish building activity and the consequent excavations to provide the city with public buildings and the residences needed by its new ruling class led to the retrieval of an enormous quantity of archaeological material that was reorganised on scholarly principles with assistance of Rodolfo Lanciani. In 1903, this able archaeologist oversaw the installation of the exhibits in an area of the Palazzo dei Conservatori (converted into a museum after it lost its official function as the headquarters of the Municipal Magistracy). Lanciani organised the exhibits on the basis of their original contexts, and his approach for the first time gave due emphasis to the excavation data. In the years of the Fascist Governatorato (1925–30) the structures of Palazzo Caffarelli (which, from the 16th century, formed a single property with Palazzo Clementino adjoining Palazzo dei Conservatori) were made an integral part of the Capitoline Museums, where numerous works previously stored in warehouses were put on public display. However the layout in what was called for a time the "Museo Mussolini," and later the Museo Nuovo, did not adopt the topographical arrangement advocated by Lanciani but sought to retrace the most significant stages in Greek art through Roman copies inspired by Greek originals. In the same years a renewed Antiquarium was erected on the Caelian hill. It contained remains reflecting the city's earliest history, from the origins to the Republican period, and objects of daily life under the empire. Only in 1956 were the museum spaces expanded with the creation of a new area of Palazzo dei Conservatori, the Braccio Nuovo. This made it possible to display material of great artistic and scholarly importance turned up by the various urban development projects from the thirties: sculptures from Republican or proto-Imperial monuments recovered on the slopes of the Capitol, when the hill was closed off, or from excavations in Largo Argentina. In the same period the collection of epigraphs was displayed in a connected underground gallery that has been recently set up.

In recent decades the progress in historical and artistic studies, research in the archives and above all study of the contents of the museums and deposits, the reassembly of sculptural groups and archaeological contexts have created a need for a better presentation of the results achieved. The work of reorganising the Capitoline Museums has led, in its first phase, to the creation of an original decentralised exhibition space, the Centrale Montemartini. At the same time new rooms were opened within the museum complex to enable the marvels of the Roman *horti*, invisible for too much time, to be exhibited to the public. The rooms of Palazzo Caffarelli already host interesting temporary exhibitions, while the Roman Garden provides a large museum setting for the equestrian statue of Marcus Aurelius and other big bronzes. (*N.G.*)

Palazzo Nuovo / Capitoline Museum

Atrium and Courtyard.

The arrangement of the rooms
on the ground floor recalls the layout
of the Roman domus, taken as the
model for patrician residences in
the 18th century. As on the outside,
with its niches surmounted with
tympana and aedicules, also the
inner portico is articulated by
openings symmetrically arranged
and divided into compartments
by architraves and columns
in travertine and plastered and
painted masonry. They contain the
larger statues and some
masterpieces from the Belvedere
collection in the Vatican that were
eventually donated to the City
of Rome, while the walls are lined
with Roman epigraphs, mostly
funerary inscriptions.

The vaulting creates unusual variations in the light and a visual atmosphere that culminates in the central part opening onto the courtyard.

We begin our visit from the right. Here we see a colossal **statue of Minerva**. It is probably based on one of the refined statues of Athene that were sculpted in Greece by Phidias in the 5th century BC, using the techniques known as chryselephantine (gold and ivory) or acrolith (with the body in marble and the drapery in fabric or bronze). The eye cavities were originally set with gemstones and metal while the holes in the zone (or belt) around the waist of the figure and the pivots still present on the breast served to attach parts made of different materials. This cult image has been attributed to the circle of Pasiteles, a sculptor from Magna Graecia, active in Rome in the 1st century BC, who sought to retrieve past technical and stylistic traditions. It may have been made for the temple of the goddess in the Iseum Campensis, in the area near the present church of Santa Maria sopra Minerva.

Halfway down, the courtyard is closed with an exedra, which scenically masks the outer wall facing the mediaeval structures of the Aracoeli. Here we find the fountain "**of Marforio**" (from Martis Forum, namely the Forum of Augustus with the Temple of Mars Ultor, from which the statue is believed to have come). The figure of the river god, originally part of the decoration of a fountain, perhaps from the Flavian period (1st century AD), was restored with

On page 116
The Cabinet of Venus
in the Capitoline Museum.

The courtyard of Palazzo Nuovo
with the fountain-statue
of Marforio and the "della Valle
Satyrs."

the attributes typical of Ocean. It became especially famous, while it still stood at the foot of the Capitol, because the Romans used to attach to it libellous attacks on the government signed with the name Pasquino. The fountain is surmounted by an inscription that commemorates the foundation of the Capitoline Museum (1734), together with a bust of the pontiff responsible. In niches at the sides are paired statues known as the **"della Valle Satyrs,"** from the palace they originally decorated. They are fine sculptures from the late Hellenistic period and represent Pan, the Greek god of the countryside and nature. They were originally located in Pompey's theatre, where they were telamones, used to support the structure.

In the courtyard stand three granite columns decorated with rows of shaven-headed priests holding attributes of the mystery religion of Isis. They may date from the renewal of the temple of the goddess in the Campus Martius by the emperor Domitian. In the museum the first formed part of a small **Egyptian Collection** that occupies a side chamber. Here we can admire one of their capitals in white marble with decorations imitating palm branches, a baboon in grey granite, sparrow-hawk in black granite and crocodile in pink granite, all dating from the last period of Egyptian independence before Alexander the Great. Among the other works is a sphinx in basanite **of the pharaoh Amasis II** (568–526 BC). The head has been deliberately damaged in an attempt to efface all memory of him (a procedure known as *damnatio memoriae*).

Continuing the visit on the right side towards the atrium, a focal point for the staircase is provided by the **colossal statue of Mars** recovered from the Forum of Nerva. This is probably a copy from the Flavian period (1st century AD) of the cult image in the Temple of Mars Ultor in the Forum of Augustus, set on the outside to replace the original damaged in a fire. Particularly notable is the very fine and richly symbolic decoration of the helmet and armour with imaginary animals.

Ground-Floor Rooms on the Right

Before going up to the *piano nobile* it is worth looking in at the three small rooms on the right facing the square, which contain epigraphic monuments of considerable interest. In the **first room** there are numerous portraits of private Roman citizens and on the right an outstanding **funerary relief** that represents, within a niche with a flat border, two living figures at the side of the deceased, a freedman (former slave) of the 1st century BC. On the wall opposite the entrance are set fragments of Roman **calendars** which represent the new year which Caesar fixed at 365 days.

The **second room** contains the **large funerary altar of Titus Statilius Aper** (= wild boar!). This is decorated on three sides while the back has a cavity for the ashes. Under the figure of the dead man an inscription records his work as a master builder in a construction firm, as also shown by the tools of his trade carved at the sides. The sepulchre belongs to the 1st century AD, a period in which cremation was in vogue. From a burial come the figures of husband and wife shown lying on the cover of the **colossal sarcophagus of Alexander Severus** in the **third room**. The representation of their features suggests a dating to the 2nd century AD. The sarcophagus is of Attic workmanship decorated on all sides with carvings in high relief representing scenes from the life of Achilles.

Gallery

You now go up the two flights of stairs of the main staircase and reach the bright gallery that connects the different rooms of the museum. Immediately striking is the **colossal statue of Hercules** that was highly admired when it was discovered during the rebuilding of the church of Sant'Agnese fuori le Mura. It was completely restored by Algardi, a great sculptor of the 17th century, who altered the composition somewhat, transforming the figure of Hercules taming a deer into Hercules slaying the Hydra. The work is a Roman reworking of a carving by Lysippus (4th century BC), who is recorded as having worked on a series of sculptures of the labours of Hercules.

The Greek sculptor probably also carved the original from which derives the Eros stringing his bow, a fine copy from the early imperial period. With an elastic rhythm, as shifting his balance, the young winged god stretches out his arms to string the bow he uses to shoot the arrows of love.

The Discobulus by Myron (circa 460 BC), a sculptor in bronze who sought tirelessly to render bodily movement in space, was the model for the ancient torso refashioned in the 18th century as the **statue of a Wounded Warrior**.

To the circle of Timotheos (a Greek artist of the 4th century BC) belongs the **statue of Leda and the Swan.** The group, widely copied from the 1st century BC, represents the erotic subject of the seduction of the mythical queen of Sparta by Zeus disguised as a swan. The Capitoline Museum is extraordinarily rich in reproductions of subjects typical of the Hellenistic period, conventionally dated from the death of Alexander the Great (323 BC). At this time, a strong interest developed in many aspects of everyday life, which were explored in all its forms, seeming even to affect the gods. An example is the statue of an **Old Woman Drunk**, one of a series of representations of the vices of degraded humanity. The Roman copy, reassembled from a number of fragments, derives from an original attested at Smyrna (Asia Minor). The refined drapery contrasts with the realistic rendering of the veins and the roughness of the skin on the skeletal body of Maronides, who clutches a wine bottle in delirious ecstasy. Also characteristic is the representation of children, often at play. A typical example is the **statuette of Heracles as a Child Strangling the Serpents**: this may contain a portrait of the young Caracalla or of Annius Verus, son of the emperor Marcus Aurelius. There are other delightful exhibits of the same kind: for example, the **Child Choking a Goose** from an original by Boethos of Rhodes (2nd century BC) and the **Child Playing with Masks**, both in the **Room of the Faun**.

Room of the Doves

To the same cultural milieu belonged the original of the **statue of a Child with a Dove** in the centre of the room. This figurative motive has a possible precedent in the carvings on the Greek funerary pillars from the 5th and 4th centuries BC. The room takes its name from the famous mosaic found in the 18th century in Hadrian's Villa at Tivoli. At that time it was called the "Room of the Miscellanies" because of the wide range of exhibits it contained, most of them from the Albani Collection, whose acquisition—as we saw above—formed the original core of the museum. The arrangement of the exhibits has suffered from only slight alterations: the portraits are still arranged on shelves along the walls, which are covered with sepulchral inscriptions. Opposite the entrance was installed the front of a **sarcophagus with the Triumph of Bacchus in India**, dating from the reign of Commodus: the god drives a cart drawn by panthers and preceded by elephants and satyrs. Under the windows that look onto the courtyard, old display cases contain documents of fundamental importance in the history of Rome, engraved forever in bronze, and the *Tabula Iliaca*, a fragment of miniature bas-relief (1st century BC) decorated with scenes of Homer's *Iliad* with captions. The **Mosaic of the Doves** was a figured panel (*emblem*) set in the middle of a pavement, also of mosaic, but decorated with simple patterns. In the panel, framed by an astragal motive, four doves perch on the rim of a bronze vase from which one drinks; under the handle there seems to be an image in relief supporting it. This is a copy from the period of Hadrian of a creation of Sosos, an artist active at Pergamum in the 2nd century BC. The subject was later repeated in early Christian art as a symbol of the soul at the spring of salvation. The remarkable skill shown in composing the tiny polychrome *tesserae* (marble and glass tiles) creates a surprisingly pictorial effect.

Less fine but highly effective is the **Mosaic of the Stage Masks** from an imperial building on the Aventine in the 2nd century AD. The two stock characters of the New Comedy—the young woman saddened by misfortune and the reflective, mocking slave—live again thanks to a mosaicist with an eye for perspective values and the interplay of light and shade.

Returning to the **gallery**, rather further along it we find two **colossal heads of deities**, of marked formal elegance, set opposite each other. These are fragments of cult statues made using the acrolithic technique, in which the exposed flesh parts were made of marble set on a wooden framework sheathed in thin sheets of metal. The way the sculptures are displayed makes it difficult to examine the rear of the heads where they were hollowed out to make them lighter. In these two figures we perhaps see all that remains of the images of Juno Regina and Apollo with the lyre, made in Rome in the 2nd century BC by the Attic sculptors Timarchides and Polycles, who received the commission from the leading families in the city.

Eros as an archer. Capitoline Museum, Rome.

Mosaic of the Doves. Capitoline Museum, Rome.

Cabinet of Venus

As you continue along the gallery you come on the right to a small polygonal platform built in the early 19th century to create an evocative setting, suggestive of a nymphaeum, for the **Venus Capitolina**. The sculpture, one of the best known and most often reproduced in the collection, is of fine marble (probably from the Greek island of Paros, given the wonderful effects of translucency in slanting light). It has come down to us perfectly preserved—the *morbidezza* of its flesh tones enhanced by recent restoration—since its ancient owner, in a moment of danger, hid it in a wall.

The goddess is represented as she emerges naked from the ritual bath, symbolised by the pitcher and cloth by her side. This iconography derives from a Hellenistic variant of the Aphrodite Pudica created by Praxiteles in the mid-4th century BC for the sanctuary of Cnidos. The Capitoline copy may have decorated a refined architectural complex from the 1st century BC or the Antoninian period.

Room of the Emperors

At the end of the arcade you turn left into a room that contains sixty-seven busts representing the Roman emperors and personages from the imperial circle ranged on a double line of shelves.

Palazzo Nuovo, Room of the Emperors.

Not all the subjects of the portraits have been definitely identified. Many are probably portraits of private citizens and were passed off as emperors in the modern period to favour the desire of collectors to possess a complete set. Many were falsified to confer on anonymous portraits the iconography of the "rarer" emperors by deducing it from portraits on coins. In the case of the Capitoline Collection, one of the richest of its type in the world, often only the bust is modern. The sculptures in this room enable us to follow the development of Roman portraiture chronologically from the Augustan age to the late ancient period, and form an illustrated abstract of the history of Rome itself. The Roman portrait developed from a variegated Greek-Hellenistic matrix. The starting point was the portraiture of Alexander the Great, who loved to have himself represented "theatrically" in different ways (as hero, as victorious general, as a philosopher, as a god): with greater realism and a close likeness when his feats were celebrated, but at other times in a more ideal way to bring out the idea of transcendence and divine assimilation. These two models inspired the portraits of Augustus in the room: the portrait of **Octavian of the "Actium type,"** set to the left of the window on the square and the **Augustus of the "Ara Pacis type,"** in front of it. In the first, so named because it dates from soon after the battle (31 BC) when the young adopted son of Caesar defeated Mark Anthony and made himself master of Rome, the hair is represented as large, dishevelled locks, the neck is twisted to one side and the face is carved with large use of chiaroscuro to create a distinctively individual likeness. The second, by contrast, represents the mature emperor, serene and aware of his authority, in which the realistic likeness is merged with a firm classical structure, as appears in the relief on the Ara Pacis. Much the same is true of the women of the imperial family. It is evident in the first **portrait of Livia**, the wife of Augustus, where there are few distinctively individual touches, with the exception of certain details, notably her hairstyle, which is often the only feature that makes an identification possible. It is also the case of the attractive **portrait of Agrippina Major** (in the corner on the right), the unfortunate bride of Germanicus. We can also admire the curls piled high on the head of the Lady Flavia, with its refined lineaments, set in front of the blind window. After this a doughnut-shaped chignon was the fashion throughout the Antonine period. A singular work is the **polychrome bust of a Roman Lady** from the reign of Alexander Severus, because it is assembled out of different parts; the hair, for example, can be removed and might have been interchangeable. In the masculine series of the emperors we can follow the development of fashions in hair and beards: the first emperors were clean-shaven, then they began to wear their hair and beard long, "in the Greek style," to look inspired and philosophically committed. In the middle of the room looms the **seated figure of Helena**, the mother of the emperor Constantine and an advocate for Christianity. Her refashioned portrait is set on a body that is a faithful copy of a famous statue of Aphrodite created in the mid-5th century BC in the circle of Phidias.

Room of the Philosophers

The next room contains a collection of the busts of poets, philosophers and orators of Greek antiquity, whose images, in Roman times and then in the Renaissance, decorated the public and private libraries, residences, villas and parks of wealthy and sensitive devotees of the arts and philosophy. Many of the portraits present are purely imaginary, intended to evoke moral and spiritual values, while those that date from the Hellenistic period and later tend to present a fairly faithful likeness of the subject.

There are numerous **herms of Homer** (immediately to the left of the entrance), on the lower shelf. His legendary blindness was said to have favoured the poet's insight into the soul and destiny of man. On the upper shelf **Socrates** appears as an ugly Silenus, a model that was created by Lysippus, fifty years after the philosopher's death, on the basis of the description given by his disciple Plato. Also of interest is the **portrait of Pythagoras** (below on the left before the exit), in which the mathematician is shown wearing a flat turban. Easily recognisable in a central position is a **two-headed herm** on which the philosopher **Epicurus**, with his arched eyebrows, is united forever with his pupil **Metrodorus**.

Among all the imperial busts, in a corner there is one that is notable by its dimensions and the quality of its workmanship, as well as being one of the most authentic portraits of the late Republican period (1st century BC). In the bust of **Cicero** we have not only the celebrated orator and writer, but also a faithful portrait of the politician and saviour of his country. Higher up, on the wall, appears a fragment of a sarcophagus with a carving in relief of the **Transportation of the Body of Meleager**, which clearly inspired Raphael in the *Deposition* in the Galleria Borghese.

Great Hall

By its breadth and monumentality the brightly lit great hall is the most representative room in the complex, planned and decorated to accommodate the sculptures visible today with a layout, unlike the previous rooms, that is more ornamental than typological. Above the walls, divided by gigantic pilasters into vertical sections articulated by aedicules and false doors, the 17th century added the extraordinary baroque coffered ceiling in which octagons, rectangles and mixed figures are interwoven with rosettes richly carved on the inside. In the middle are the arms of the Pamphilj pope, Innocent X, who was responsible for completing the palace. Note also the large portal (an arch with two winged victories modelled in stucco), made in the first half of the 18th century, which communicates with the gallery.

In the middle of the great hall, there are two *pendant* pieces: paired **Centaurs** (mythological creatures, half horse half man) found in the 18th-century excavations of Hadrian's Villa at Tivoli. The sculptures, in a rare and very fine marble (*bigio morato*), were signed by Aristeas and Papias, artists of Aphrodisias, a city of Asia Minor which had a school of skilful copiers of Greek sculpture, who were kept busy by their demanding Roman clients. The search for metallic effects in the rendering of details in these replicas, which date from the reign of Hadrian (2nd century AD), as well as the handling of form and the colouring of the marble suggest they derive from bronze originals of the Hellenistic period, which loved representations that were richly anecdotal and moralistic. The young Centaur trots cheerfully and holds his prey; the elderly Centaur, by contrast, is weary and troubled by the pangs of love: originally a cupid fastened his arms behind his back.

Next to the large central window, from which you can look out over the square, there stands the **statue of an Amazon of the "Capitoline**

type," representing one of the mythical warlike women especially honoured in Asia Minor. The sources recount that in the second half of the 5th century BC the greatest Greek artists (including Phidias and Polycletes) vied to produce the official model of the Amazon—no longer as fierce warriors but wounded and veiled with melancholy—to be dedicated in the shrine of Artemis at Ephesus. So there may be an echo of the winning model by Polycletes, especially in the rhythmic coherence typical of the sculptor, in this replica, signed by a neo-Attic artist named Sosikles, but rather heavily altered in the 18th century.

Room of the Faun

Our visit concludes with the last two rooms, where the exhibits are displayed on aesthetic principles, with the sculptural work in the centre showcased as a "masterpiece." This work, in a valuable *rosso antico* marble, comes from Hadrian's Villa and was acquired for the museum by Benedict XIV. Delicate 18th-century restoration, which entailed numerous additions, has not however changed the ancient image greatly. This is a model that was very widespread in Hellenistic times, when a taste developed for Dionysian subjects with bucolic and rural settings. The **Faun**, half animal, half man, with a deerskin tied over its shoulders, seems to be executing a dance step. The figure was of the kind used to decorate Roman gardens (*horti*). The meticulous rendering of anatomical details (note the rippling, tensed muscles), the sockets in the inebriated face, which were set with vivid gemstone eyes and brows made of metal, again show this is a copy of a bronze and can be ascribed, like the Centaurs in the Great Hall, to the school of Aphrodisias mentioned above.

Among the epigraphs on the walls is the especially noteworthy bronze table (on the right side) of the ***Lex de imperio Vespasiani***, a decree which conferred special powers on the emperor in the 1st century AD. By reading and commenting on these words, not engraved but cast in bronze, Cola di Rienzo kindled the populace of Rome to emulate the ancient grandeur of the city.

Room of the Gladiator

This room takes its name from the central sculpture, the **Dying Warrior**. When, in 1734, it was acquired from the Ludovisi Collection, the figure was erroneously interpreted as a gladiator falling on his shield and became probably the best known work in the collection, frequently copied in engravings and drawings.

The Galatian is surrounded by other copies of considerable quality. The **Wounded Amazon** leads us back to the model sculpted by Phidias for the competition at Ephesus, by the delicate and luminous handling of the drapery, in which it is similar to the Amazons that appear in the decoration of the Parthenon.

There is also a very fine **statue of Hermes** which the emperor Hadrian ordered should be given the face of **Antinous**, the young man he loved. The **Satyr Resting** is one of the best known replicas of the original by Praxiteles (4th century BC). This image of the young satyr, its pointed ears set amid thick gilded locks, lounging against a tree trunk, must have been an ornament for a wood or a nymphaeum. Near the window, the delightful rococo group of **Love and Psyche** symbolize the tender union of the human soul with divine love, a theme that goes back to the platonic philosophy and was immensely popular in early Hellenistic art. (*N.G.*)

The Galatians Vanquished. The Triumph over the Barbarians: From Pergamum to Rome

The Dying Warrior. Capitoline Museum, Rome.

This was the title of a recent exhibition which presented, recomposed for the first time, two exceptional sculptural groups from different Roman museums. It enabled scholars and the general public to understand the famous votive bronze by Epigonus installed in the court of the shrine of Athens at Pergamum. This commemorated the decisive victory of Attalus I over the Galatians (as the Greeks called the Celts, the "Gauls" of the Romans, who had settled in a central region of what is now Turkey), at a battle fought at the river Caicus in about 240 BC. Whether the figures were originally placed, as is most likely, on a circular base with a large commemorative inscription, or on a long rectangular pedestal together with other dying figures, their arrangement in three-dimensional space must have offered a dynamic sequence of points of view from 360 degrees, confirming the Hellenistic sculptors' concern for scenic effects in a theatre of the senses that here attained the most intense pathos. The dramatic focus of the monument was clearly the group with the Galatian committing suicide, pictured with extraordinary expressive power at the moment when he sinks the sword in his neck after bravely wounding his wife to death: his only hope to escape capture and slavery. The dying Galatian is represented with his characteristic attributes (shield, the *torques* or neck ring, heroic nakedness, moustache and the locks of his hair streaked with chalk water to strike fear into the Mediterranean enemy), and with the wound clearly visible, as he fights against pain to the last. Disquietingly modern is the typically Hellenistic decision not to celebrate the victors but the barbarians vanquished, representing pride amid human suffering, regardless of ethnic differences. It has been credibly suggested that these copies, in Asian marble, found in the Villa Ludovisi in Rome, where Caesar's summer residence stood, were commissioned by the dictator from a workshop in Pergamum to symbolically evoke in a private context his conquest of Western Gaul in 46–43 BC. (*N.G.*)

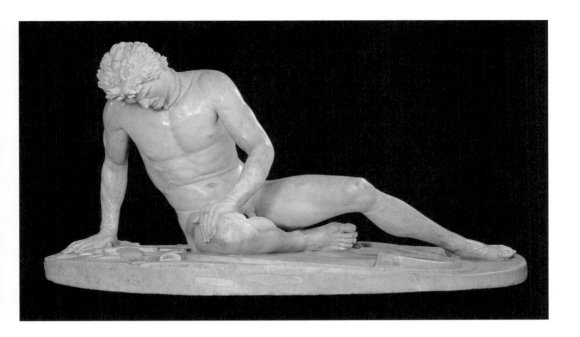

Palazzo dei Conservatori

<u>Courtyard.</u> The right side of the courtyard retains traces of the ogival arches that gave access to the collection of statuary in the earliest collections. This courtyard, as was usual in all noble palaces, was used to display works of ancient art. On the right wall are set fragments of the **colossal acrolith of Constantine** (313–324 AD), recovered in the 15th century in the west apse of the basilica of Maxentius in the Forum, which was completed by the emperor. The statue, which showed him enthroned, had only the exposed flesh parts made of marble. These were mounted on a frame of wood and masonry and sheathed in drapery made of gilt bronze or sheets of precious coloured marble.

Constantine is here represented as a god, uncontaminated by the outer world, in frozen abstract forms comprising the features of his face, which stand out starkly in their marked realism (the aquiline nose, prominent chin and long, thin lips). The face is dominated by the enormous eyes which, in their fixity, seem to gaze beyond the visible world.

On the left side of the courtyard are arranged carvings from a temple that Antoninus Pius dedicated in 145 AD to his adoptive father Hadrian, who was deified after his death: its remains are still visible, incorporated into the Palazzo della Borsa (stock exchange building) in Piazza di Pietra. Plinths with trophies of arms alternate with bases with personifications of the **Provinces** vanquished, recognisable by their attributes. At the far end of the courtyard, a portico added in the 18th century, contains **Two Prisoners** carved in an elegant marble (*bigio morato*), which have affinities with the series in the Forum built by Trajan, the conqueror of the Dacians. Between them is set the singular group of the **Goddess Rome**: this figure was assembled out of sculptural fragments from different periods and styles in the mid-16th century by Cardinal Cesi. The work testifies to the taste of the time for bold combinations (also practised by the Romans in antiquity), and restorations that were often assemblages or distortions that completely changed the significance of the original.

Main Staircase (First and Second Landings)

In the vestibule of the palace there is the very fine original plaque recording the controversial donation by Pope Sixtus IV of the Lateran bronzes. You then go up to the **first landing** of the monumental staircase, where the 16th century affixed four large **historical reliefs from the imperial period**, today enhanced by the effective lighting. The first three are part of a set of eleven panels, eight of which were reused in decorating the attic of the Arch of Constantine. They come from official monuments dedicated to Marcus Aurelius between 176 and 180 AD. Continuing up the staircases, on the right you find a panel of the emperor making sacrifices at the Temple of Capitoline Jupiter, here in one of its most detailed depictions. The following reliefs commemorate his triumph and his mildness to the vanquished, in an attitude like that of the bronze statue in the square. The fourth panel, originally part of a public monument in honour of Hadrian, represents the emperor entering the city. On the wall of the **second landing** (where the vault is embellished with refined stucco decorations) there is one of two panels that originally decorated what was known as the "Arco di Portogallo" on the Via Lata (now the Via del Corso). This was a late-antique monument made out of scavenged materials and destroyed in the 17th century to widen the road. In the relief, the emperor Hadrian presides over the distribution of food to Roman children.

Apartment of the Conservatori

On the first floor we find the state rooms of the palace which accommodated the magistrates known as the Conservatori. The fresco cycles and sumptuous decorations—the intaglio work and painted decorations on the ceilings, carved doors, stucco decorations and 18th-century tapestries —are

On page 128
Colossal head of Constantine, after the recent restoration. Capitoline Museums, Palazzo dei Conservatori, Rome.

the result of additions at different times over the centuries. However, the theme of the decoration was always consistent, being centred on the principal and most striking events of monarchical and Republican Rome, so conferring a unity on the decoration of the chambers and testifying to their enduring symbolic significance through the exaltation of the civic virtues.

Room of the Horatii and the Curiatii

The large chamber, which acquired its present dimensions after Michelangelo remodelled the palace, was originally used for meetings of the Consiglio Pubblico and is still in use for important ceremonies. In the late 16th century the Cavalier d'Arpino, a leading representative of Mannerism in Rome, was commissioned to paint a series of highly expressive works evoking the legendary history of the origins of Rome, as related by Livy in his *Histories*. The painter conceived the frescoes as a tapestry unfurled on the walls, in which the episodes are separated by vertical bands decorated with festoons of fruit and flowers, trophies of arms and lustral vases. Along the base runs a frieze of imitation marble with monochrome medallions depicting events in Roman history correlated with the subjects above. On the short sides of the chamber a heavy red curtain supported by telamones drapes the scenes, with cupids exhibiting the emblems of the Roman people.

At the far end of the room, the first fresco depicts *Faustulus Discovering the She-Wolf* with the twins on the banks of the Tiber, in a spacious sunny landscape. This is followed, in order of execution, on the left wall by the *Battle of the Romans against the Inhabitants of Veii and Fidene*, where the artist reveals his skill in spatial organisation and dramatic expression. The fallen warrior in the foreground contains an echo of the dying Galatian in the Capitoline. Nearby is the *Battle between the Horatii and the Curiatii* (1612–13)—a decisive event in the conflict between Rome and Alba Longa for supremacy in Latium, which gives the room its name. In exalting the value of the individual hero, the painter sublimates the *virtus* of a whole people. The last frescoes were painted over twenty years later with the help of pupils and seem to have lost freshness and originality, though the colouring is harmonious: on the right wall two works represent *Romulus Fixing the Boundaries of Roma Quadrata*, and *Numa Pompilio Founding the Cult of the Vestals*. On the shorter side of the room adjoining them is the *Rape of the Sabine Maidens*. Then, to "inhabit" this wonderful setting, came **Urban VIII** (sculpted in marble between 1635 and 1640 by Gian Lorenzo Bernini and assistants) and **Innocent X** (cast in bronze by Algardi between 1645 and 1650), set opposite one another, solemn and vivid presences, their hands raised in blessing.

Room of the Captains

You pass through two doors, their leaves richly adorned with reliefs, and enter what used to be the audience chamber; it is now called the Room of the Captains because of the numerous commemorative plaques, honourary statues and baroque busts of generals of the armies of the Church who distinguished themselves in war. Among the military leaders represented,

particularly noteworthy are **Marcantonio Colonna**, who commanded the papal fleet that fought against the Turks at Lepanto in 1571 and Carlo Barberini, brother of Pope Urban VIII, represented by a re-used Roman statue of an armoured figure, restored by Algardi (who added legs, arms and shield), while Bernini produced the very effective portrait.

Of particular interest in this room are the large frescoes painted in the closing decades of the 16th century by Tommaso Laureti, a pupil of Sebastiano del Piombo. They embody the figurative language of late Roman Mannerism, with frequent allusions to the work of Michelangelo and Raphael. The virtue and courage of the ancient Romans are celebrated with vivid colouring and monumental forms, with scenes from the history of the early republic. The end wall, in front of which the magistrates known as the Conservatori sat in judgment, significantly represents the Justice of Brutus, who had no hesitation in sentencing his own sons to death. The fresco decorating the wall on the left celebrates the *Victory over the Tusculans at Lake Regillus*; that on the right represents *Horatius Cocles* defending the Sublician bridge during the siege of the Etruscan king Porsenna, who appears on the wall with the entrance before *Mutius Scaevola*.

Cavalier d'Arpino,
Battle between the Horatii and the Curiatii (1612–13), details.

Room of the Triumphs

This room preserves the most ancient wooden ceilings in the palace (1568), with the brilliance of their colouring and the carvings of very fine trophies of arms recently restored. Underneath it runs a frescoed frieze, painted by the pupils of Daniele da Volterra, which gives the room its name. It celebrates the triumph of the consul L. Aemilius Paulus over Perseus, king of Macedonia (167 BC). The painters depict the unfolding of the procession, following in some detail the description by the classical historian Plutarch but drawing formally on ancient reliefs. The backdrop to the stage depicts the victor's ritual ascent to the Capitol, with an interplay between past and present, because the Temple of Capitoline Jupiter has been curiously replaced by the façade of the Palazzo dei Conservatori, as remodelled by Giacomo Della Porta with the insertion of the large window and central balcony. Painted specially for this room were the works by Piazza (a *Deposition*, painted on slate, 1614) and G. Francesco Romanelli (*Santa Francesca Romana*, 1638), both pervaded by an evocative handling of light. The large early painting by Pietro da Cortona of *Alexander's Victory over Darius* was painted in the mid-16th century to celebrate Alessandro Sacchetti, the commander of the papal troops, who commissioned many of the artist's works.

This room contains three ancient bronzes. In the centre it is the **Spinarius**, a small sculpture that depicts a boy drawing a thorn from his foot.

The singular and graceful pose of the figure, caught in this unusual gesture, made this one of the ancient works most widely studied and imitated in the Renaissance. It is an eclectic creation of the 1st century BC, combining different formal models: on the delicate body of Hellenistic derivation (3rd–2nd century BC) the artist has set a head modelled in the severe style of Greek works from the mid-5th century BC.

Spinarius. Capitoline Museums, Palazzo dei Conservatori, Rome.

The Capitoline Brutus. Capitoline Museums, Palazzo dei Conservatori, Rome.

The silver-eyed statue of **Camillus** is fashioned in the classical style of the 1st century AD. It was long identified as a "Gypsy Woman" because of the soft and elegant hairstyle, feminine features and soft drapery. This young member of a religious cult (*camillus*) must have held a small cup for ritual libations in his right hand. But the absolute masterpiece that all pause to admire is undoubtedly the **Capitoline Brutus**.

Room of the She-Wolf

Ever since the mid-16th century the **She-Wolf** has stood here, even when this chamber was originally a three-arched loggia facing the city (traces of this remain on the outside wall). It was moved here from the 15th-century façade of the building when Michelangelo remodelled it, at the same time also placing the fragments of the Fasti Consulares and Fasti Triumphales,

brought here from the Forum, on the end wall of the courtyard. They were reassembled with a fair degree of fidelity in this room, to the detriment of a valuable fresco cycle by the Bolognese painter Jacopo Ripanda painted under the papacy of Julius II (1503–1513). The scenes are hard to interpret now (though the triumph of Lucius Aemilius Paulus has been reliably identified), having been further damaged by the insertion of two celebratory plaques that left only four scenes intact. A valuable aid in reconstructing Roman history, the **Fasti Consulares** and **Fasti Triumphales** are inscriptions that restore the lists of the magistrates from the foundation of the Republic and of those who were also awarded a triumph from the days of Romulus. The list came to an end with the reign of Augustus because the plaques were set on the walls of an arch dedicated in 19 BC to Augustus in memory of his victorious campaign against the Parthians.

Eyes that Reflect Values

One of the most famous portraits of antiquity is the magnificent Capitoline Brutus, so-called because 16th-century antiquarians identified it as a portrait of Brutus Junius, the first Roman consul who unhesitatingly sentenced his own sons to death, after expelling the tyrant-king Tarquinius Superbus. He was famed as an example of justice in the highest position in the state. The identification was based on comparison with the likenesses on coins of another Junius Brutus, the assassin of Caesar, and also the figure's *gravitas*, the sense of commitment and ideal tension, an ideological quality attributed to the patricians. This sense of pride is particularly striking in the extraordinarily expressive force of the face, achieved through a physiognomic study of character—with the marks left by time on the vigorous cheekbones and spacious forehead, and the thin, compressed lips—and the refined workmanship: the vivid, penetrating eyes of ivory and glass paste are ancient. However, considerable problems surround the identification and interpretation of this work. The iconography, in some ways related to Greek portraits of poets and philosophers, is interpreted by the Roman culture of the Republican age in the 4th and 3rd centuries BC (the head is also similar to that of Velthur Velcha frescoed in the Tomb of the Shields at Tarquinius). Few other bronze portraits have survived from this period: there is a splendid example from San Giovanni Lipioni, now in the Bibliothèque Nationale in Paris. Some scholars, however, largely through a study of the modelling of the hair, believe this is a creation of the Augustan age, the celebration of a *vir illustris*, perhaps even Romulus, as part of the systematic recovery of the ancient glory. (*N.G.*)

Room of the Geese

This room has recovered the agreeable decorative unity desired by the Farnese pope Paul III (1534–1549), whose traditional emblems of the lily and the lightning bolt appear in the shields on the wall by the window. Of great interest is the frieze in which elegant patterns frame scenes of ancient games set against backdrops of imaginary or real landscapes, such as the view of Piazza del Campidoglio with the Church of Aracoeli before it was restructured under the Farnese pope. The room takes its name from two **small bronze geese** from ancient times, traditionally interpreted as the legendary geese of the Capitol whose cackling raised the alarm and saved Rome from a Gallic invasion. There is also an 18th-century **portrait of Michelangelo**, in bronze on a marble bust, derived from one made by Daniele da Volterra from the artist's death mask. As well there is a small replica of the singular Hellenistic **cult statue** in the **Temple of Artemis** at Ephesus. Its extremities were made of bronze and its body of marble: from it hang a bull's testicles as a symbol of fertility, together with figures of animals and bees because the goddess was also their patron. In the room there is a refined **shelf** with a cult function (4th century AD): round the border runs a band of decoration **with scenes from the life of Achilles**. The original element was reused in the decoration of the church of Aracoeli painted in the 13th century by the Cosmati workshop, which also executed the fine intarsia of coloured marble and glass paste. Finally there is a striking **head of Medusa**, sculpted by Bernini in 1630: her twofold nature, human and monstrous, is emphasised by the different degrees of finish of the marble, left rough on the serpent hair and smooth on the face.

Room of the Eagles

The refined decoration of this small chamber dates from the same period as that of the previous room. The frieze, framed by grotesques, represents interesting sights of the Rome of the age, such as Piazza del Campidoglio, where the equestrian statue of Marcus Aurelius had just arrived and work had begun on remodelling the palaces. The title of the room, formerly the Wardrobe of the Conservatori, derives from two imperial sculptures set by the door on columns of *cipollino* marble.

Room of the Tapestries

From these small rooms you pass into a chamber that contains some of the earliest decorations of the palace: the splendid wooden coffered ceiling and frescoes (1544) from the circle of Daniele da Volterra, in which the representation of famous ancient sculptures, like the Hercules and the Laocoon, at that time recently rediscovered, alternate with scenes from the life of Scipio Africanus and the mythical loves of Jove. In the 18th century the room was entirely renewed to install the canopy over the papal throne. It was then decided to cover the walls with precious tapestries (woven in the Roman workshop of San Michele) with images of works preserved in the Capitol: the painting by Rubens of *Romulus and Remus Suckled by the She-Wolf* and *Cardinal Cesi's Goddess Rome*. Corvi's preparatory cartoon showed the personifications of the Tiber and Aniene set at her feet.

Room of Hannibal

The next room has the most ancient ceiling in the palace and the still intact original fresco decorations. They are attributed to the workshop of Jacopo Ripanda (1508–13). The cycle is rich in antiquarian interest and testifies to the fascination with classical antiquity characteristic of the Bolognese school. It recounts episodes of the Punic wars. There is the well-known scene of *Hannibal in Italy*: the Carthaginian commander, mounted on one of the legendary elephants, is ingenuously represented as wearing an eastern turban. This room also contains the splendid crater vase of **Mithridates Eupator**, king of Pontus (120–63 BC), found in Nero's villa at Anzio. It must have been brought to Italy among the spoils of war by Sulla or Pompey and, therefore, the vase evokes the sumptuous triumphal processions that followed the campaigns of conquest in the East, when the most precious works of art taken from the enemy were carried in procession.

Sale Castellani

Set at the end of the route through the museum, which unfolds within the suite known as the Appartament of the Conservatori, these two rooms contain a valuable collection of ancient materials donated to the Musei Capitolini by Augusto Castellani, a famous goldsmith and collector who lived in Rome in the second half of the 19th century.

They consist of over 700 items from the most important archaeological sites of Etruria, Latium and Magna Graecia and cover a time span from the 8th to the 4th century BC. Outstanding among the exhibits is the **Krater of Aristonothos**, a masterpiece of archaic ceramic. On one side the decoration represents the Homeric episode of the blinding of Polyphemus, on the other a naval battle, perhaps a clash between Etruscans and Greeks.

Main Staircase (Second and Third Landing)

Returning to the main staircase you find, on the **second landing**, in a room destined to the Mediaeval collections, a statue of the enthroned figure of **Charles of Anjou**, a senator of Rome in the late 13th century. The statue is not documented but is unanimously attributed to the Roman period of **Arnolfo di Cambio** on the basis of historical data (the artist was in the service of the king of Sicily) as well as stylistic grounds. Arriving at the **third landing** of the staircase, which leads to the art gallery, on the wall at the left we find the second of the historical reliefs with subjects related to the reign of Hadrian from the Arch of Portugal. This is the **Apotheosis of Sabina**, borne heavenwards by a female winged figure (Aeternitas) from the flames that consume her body. The emperor Hadrian is present at this deification of the wife whom he never loved together with a youthful personification of the Campus Martius, where the event took place.

Affixed on the wall opposite each other are **panels** in *opus sectile* of **tigers attacking calves**. They are two of the few surviving fragments (two other remarkable pieces are in Palazzo Massimo alle Terme) of the splendid inlaid polychrome marble decoration of the basilica of Junius Bassus, built by the consul in the area of Santa Maria Maggiore in the second quarter of the 4th century AD as the meeting place for a pagan congregation, hence not with a religious function.

At this point we find ourselves in front of the entrance to the art gallery (**Pinacoteca Capitolina**), housed in the rooms and gallery restored on the second level of the museum complex.

Relief from the Arch of
Portugal. Capitoline Museums,
Palazzo dei Conservatori, Rome.

Panel in coloured marble from
the Basilica of Junius Bassus
representing a tiger attacking a
calf. Capitoline Museums,
Palazzo dei Conservatori, Rome.

Gallery and the Sale degli Horti

Descending the main staircase to the second landing, we pass through the **Sale dei Fasti Moderni**, whose walls are lined with inscriptions recording the names of the civic magistrates who succeeded each other in the government of Rome from 1640 on. From here we enter the Gallery and the Sale degli Horti, where we find a section newly installed on museological principles which faithfully reflect the original display commissioned by Rodolfo Lanciani. The setting enhances the refinement of the marbles and the artistic quality of the ancient statues which once decorated the *horti*, residential complexes immersed in gardens on the margins of the monumental center of Rome, prestigious residences of the most eminent aristocratic families in late republican times, which then passed into the ownership of the emperors and were often absorbed into the gardens of the patrician villas in modern times. The finds mostly came to light in late 19th-century excavations due to the building boom after Rome became the capital of the unified Italian state, and were saved from the ravenous antiquarian market, which would have dispersed the heritage of the past.

Besides the refined facings in coloured marbles and gems, there are two absolute masterpieces that come from the Horti Lamiani. The first is the sensuous **Esquiline Venus**, represented in the act of binding her hair before immers-

The Esquiline Venus, detail. Musei Capitolini, Gallery of the Horti Lamiani, Rome.

Statue of Marsyas. Capitoline Museums, Palazzo dei Conservatori, Rome.

Following pages
The new exhibition display in the Gallery of the Horti Lamiani.

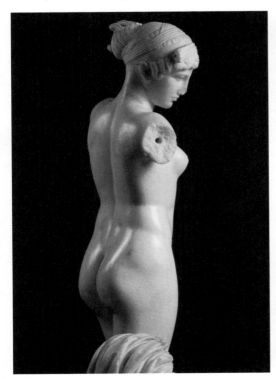

ing herself in fragrant rosewater; an Egyptian vase covered with a soft cloth and with a cobra wound around it suggests an identification with Isis-Aphrodite, in the religious syncretism of Hellenized Egypt. The second is the **group of Commodus as Hercules flanked by two Tritons**, notable for its crisp modelling and refined details. It is well preserved, because it was concealed in ancient times in an underground chamber on the Esquiline. Two tritons, that survive of a larger group, mark the apotheosis of the emperor-god in the guise of Hercules, having assimilated his attributes—the lion's pelt, club and the apples of the Hesperides—which evoke the labours of the hero. The bust rests, apparently "precariously," on an allegory whose symbolism reveals the celebratory purpose of the group.

From the Horti of Maecenas comes the splendid **statue of Marsyas**, a copy from the Augustan age of a Hellenistic original. The work represents the satyr Marsyas, who found the flute of Athena and had the audacity to challenge Apollo to a musical competition with the Muses for judges. The god succeeded in winning the competition with a subterfuge and inflicted cruel punishment on his rash opponent by flaying him alive. The veining of the *pavonazzetto* marble was skilfully exploited to render the bared flesh, while the position of the figure lashed to a pine, with muscles tensed and suffering face, a true masterpiece of expressionistic art, inspired numerous crucifixions.

Exedra of Marcus Aurelius

The large new glass-roofed room built within what was called the "Roman Garden" of the Palazzo dei Conservatori is the latest prestigious architectural

The Exedra of Marcus Aurelius.

Fragments of the colossal bronze statue of Constantine. Musei Capitolini, Exedra of Marcus Aurelius, Rome.

project to be completed in the Capitoline museum complex. The aim of the project by Carlo Aymonino was to create a bright and spacious "protected" area which could be used for the outstanding monumental works from the Temple of Capitoline Jupiter and restore to the great **equestrian statue of Marcus Aurelius** the aura of its historical but now unadvisable location in the open air of the square. The emperor-philosopher (161–180 AD) is represented as advanced in years and making a gesture of pacification to epitomize the wars he undertook in the defense of the frontiers of the empire. The stoicism of his thought illuminates his figure with serene austerity, a majestic charisma. The bronze group, originally belonging to a triumphal monument and perhaps already gilded in antiquity, is made from a number of different pieces welded together. It only escaped being melted down because in the Middle Ages it was believed to represent Constantine in the act of blessing and so was mistaken for a symbol of Christianity.

The equestrian statue, always admirable, was first placed on the Lateran and then the Capitol. Artists of all ages have been inspired by it, starting from Donatello. Now around this symbol gravitate the most ancient archaeological relics of the Capitolium as well as some of the large bronzes, the original nucleus of the Capitoline collections. The elements of the **colossal statue of Constantine** formed part of the Lateran treasure in the Middle Ages and, as is said above, reached the Capitol in 1471 with the donation of Sixtus IV. The head, a masterpiece of ancient bronze sculpture, impressive both by its size and the intensity of its features, was associated with the portraits of Constantine in the last period of his life. The statue was assembled out of separate parts; the gilding may be original. To the same complex also belong the hand which supported the globe, a celestial symbol of earthly dominion. This work, like the acrolite (meteorite) in the courtyard, was in harmony with the imposing architectural backdrops of the period and with the late-antique ideal of an emperor directly in contact with the supernatural.

Another notable exhibit in the Exedra is the gleaming **statue of Hercules in gilt bronze**, recovered in the area of the Forum Boarium adjacent to the mediaeval church of Santa Maria in Cosmedin, under the pontificate of Sixtus IV. The sculpture, not exempt from reworking, has been dated by some scholars as late as the 3rd century AD. However, a widely accepted theory sees it as the cult image of a round temple dedicated in the second century AD by Scipio Aemilianus to the Greek hero, here represented holding the apples of the Hesperides in allusion to the family's Hispanic achievements. The proportions and strong modelling of the body reveal that the sculptor was inspired by Greek originals of the 4th century BC, close to the style of Lysippus. A recent conjecture suggests it was directly derived from the cast of a bronze of that period.

Site of the Temple of Jupiter

The temple of Jupiter Optimus Maximus was also dedicated to Juno and Minerva (the Capitoline Triad) in the first year of the Roman Republic on 13 September 509 BC. Thereafter it was rebuilt several times. The monumental remains of the wall of its podium, made from blocks of cappellaccio (tufa) are surrounded by the most ancient archaeological remains in the Museums. Besides the graphic reconstructions and the remains found in the most recent excavations on the Capitoline Hill, which revealed human settlement from the middle Bronze Age, a necropolis from the Iron Age and the last remains from the built-up area obliterated by the massive work undertaken for the construction of the temple, there is an interesting terracotta fragment of a wounded warrior from the decoration of a temple on the Esquiline, which dates from the 5th century BC, and various items from the royal period recovered in the sacred precinct of the Forum Boarium, near the 16th century church of Sant'Omobono. From the

archaic temples that stood on the slopes of the Capitol, not far from the Tiber, come terracotta plaques of two felines "affronted" (set heraldically face to face) in the decoration from the pediment and the terracotta acroterial group of the presentation of Hercules to Olympus by a goddess, traditionally identified as Athena.

On the other side of the building, recent restoration has led to the reopening of some exhibition spaces. In a room of Palazzo Clementino, preceded by ancient rooms, the **Medagliere Capitolino** (Medal Collection) has an effective new display and has been reopened to the public. The long passage leads into the adjoining rooms of Palazzo Caffarelli, which contains the museum cafeteria and a large terrace that overlooks the domes and roofs of Rome, and above this the more compact spaces enlivened by frequent and interesting temporary exhibitions. As you go towards the exit you will see numerous terracotta figures that have finally been recomposed into the very fine decoration of the pediment of a Roman temple of the Republican period. (*N.G.*)

A view of the site of the Temple of Jupiter.

Acroterial relief with Heracles and the sea monster from a late Republican temple on the Caelian Hill. Capitoline Museums, Palazzo dei Conservatori, Rome.

Terracotta Gods

The vitality of the world's most ancient museum complex is shown by its ability to continue to act as cultural driving force, largely through its promotion of studies and research that enhance the value of its legacy. In this way, careful exploration in the warehouses of the Antiquarium Comunale—a facility crucial to the understanding of ancient Rome, but unfortunately now closed for some decades—has made it possible to complete the scholarly reconstruction of the decoration of a pediment, known as the "pediment of San Gregorio." This is because the fragments were discovered at the end of the 19th century in Via San Gregorio on the slopes of the Caelian and have reliably been identified as belonging to a temple from the late Republican period on the hill.
The tympanum was decorated with carvings in high relief and represented the scene of a sacrifice to Mars (perhaps the god to whom the building was dedicated), supported by a female deity. The ceremony, performed by a magistrate wearing a toga, involved the sacrifice of animals led by attendants in two separate lines that converge from the sides on the centre.
A small but splendid acroterial relief, recently rediscovered, seems to represent the myth of Heracles in the Troad, where he freed Hesione from the sea monster. This was attached to the cornice that ran along the roof eaves. Skilful restoration has revealed the lively polychrome decoration of not only the figures but all the elements, bringing the scene back to life in all its complex articulation. (*N.G.*)

The She-Wolf without the Twins

The Capitoline Wolf:
an unusual view.

Capitoline She-Wolf.
Capitoline Museums, Palazzo
dei Conservatori, Rome.
The She-Wolf was restored
a number of times in antiquity.
After being moved from the
Lateran (where it was the
symbol of justice) to the Capitol
in 1471, the twins were added to
record their miraculous nursing.

We have already seen the importance of the She-Wolf in the history of the city of Rome, of which it has become the undisputed symbol, even of the city's soccer team. The research that underpinned in an exhibition confirmed the independence of the creation that, as shown by the almost heraldic and individual pose, had nothing to do with the twins and with the legend of the city's origins. The bronze is a fine piece of Etruscan workmanship—the earth found inside it used for casting seems to come from the valley of the Tiber between Orvieto and Rome, the lead of the alloy from Sardinian mines—made by skilled craftsmen who had devoted careful study to contemporary work in Magna Graecia. Perhaps it was from a workshop in Veii because of similarities with the acroterial terracotta statues found in the temple at Portonaccio and traditionally attributed to Vulca. It can be dated, on stylistic grounds, to the end of the first quarter of the 5th century BC. The muzzle seems modelled from life (with still visible the imprints of the artist's fingers and spatula on the terracotta mould), while the skeleton showing under the skin testifies to a figurative naturalism, not yet pervaded by the anatomical perfection typical of the period preceding classical idealism. There is a degree of decorative stylisation characteristic of the late-archaic period in the fur of the mane and along the back. (*N.G.*)

The Medagliere Capitolino: A Casket of Wonders

Founded in 1872 thanks to a legacy of ancient and modern coins and precious stones, the Medagliere Capitolino was immediately increased by a rich donation made by Augusto Castellani, a member of a famous Roman family of goldsmiths, who also curated the first exhibition as director of the Capitoline Museums. The Medagliere has absorbed various other collections and been enriched by finds of hoards and treasure that have added numerous coins and examples of glyptic art (engraved gemstones) from different periods, brought here from the excavations conducted by the Civic Archaeological Commission (1872–1925) and the Fascist Governatorato (1925–1939).

As demolition went ahead for the construction of Via dei Fori Imperiali in 1933, a stir was caused by the fortuitous discovery of what was called the hoard of Via Alessandrina: seventeen kilos of gold in the form of coins and jewels. It was added to the collection only after a long lawsuit with the heirs of the antiquarian who had concealed the hoard. In the same years there was also the interesting discovery of the hoard of the Capitol in the underground passage linking the Capitoline Palaces. Acquisitions and donations in the 20th century increa-

Goth brooches in the form of eagles. Capitoline Museums, Medagliere Capitolino, Rome.

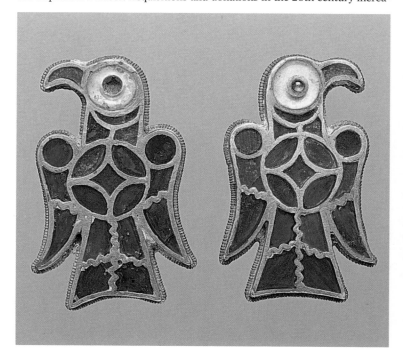

sed the collection of medals, which is an important part the history of the Capitoline Museums, some issued by eminent members of the Roman Senate, and lately of the moulds in red sulphur from the later 18th century, made from the cameos and carved gems in the Boncompagni Ludovisi Collection.

So despite the heterogeneous origins of this collection (on the antiquarian market, in collections, and in archaeological excavations), in a single room, it is possible to retrace the history of Roman coin from the *aes grave* to the most precious Republican coinages, to the imperial gold coins and the interesting late ancient issues, with their notable economic implications, clearly explained by the hypermedial information system. However, the eye is attracted above all to some of the famous figures of ancient Rome, the striking episodes of its history, the lost monuments of the city, and is fascinated by the quality of the forms and workmanship of the carving on the coloured gemstones, where refined portraits alternate with mythical scenes and delightful heraldic creatures set in elegant frames. A masterpiece of goldsmith's work from the imperial period is the gold brooch, with an engraved amethyst and ivy-leaf pendants, from the accoutrements in the sarcophagus of Crepereia Tryphaena, found during work on the construction of the Law Courts. Also notable is the Goth pair of *fibulae* with eagles, executed in the *cloisonné* technique, with irises made of rock crystal and the pupils of garnets. No less interesting are the modern jewels, such as the medallions in minute mosaic and the senatorial necklaces. (*N.G.*)

Sestertius of Trajan with the Circus Maximus, commemorating of the extensive building projects carried out by the emperor, 113 AD. Capitoline Museums, Medagliere Capitolino, Rome.

Sardonyx cameo with Livia veiled. Capitoline Museums, Medagliere Capitolino, Rome.

Archaeology on the Capitol

<u>Underground Passage.</u> If you come from the Palazzo Nuovo or Palazzo dei Conservatori, you can descend under the ground and discover the ancient buildings that once stood below the square and Palazzo Senatorio. In the late 1930s excavations were made in the area between the pedestal of the statue of Marcus Aurelius and the façade of the building to add an underground passage. The work revealed, at a depth of about eight metres, the existence of an ancient road running between the slopes of the Arx and of the Capitol, supported by walls made out of large blocks of tuff. The road came from the Campus Martius and was flanked by brick buildings rom the imperial period (the last of which

had pillars with brackets supporting balconies) and it must then have turned towards the Capitol, skirting the Temple of Veiovis and the Tabularium.

Galleria Lapidaria

The unusual setting of the 130 inscriptions in this gallery (known as the Galleria di Congiunzione), which historically houses the Capitoline's Epigraphic Collection, evokes the image of an ancient Roman Consular road under a night sky, in which the constellations have been replaced by the letters of the Greek and Latin alphabets. Besides making the ancient texts comprehensible in their different languages, the display reconstructs and compares the various aspects of Roman history, society and civilization: burial, religion, law, work and play, roads and aqueducts, the militia and the Roman aristocracy. Many epigraphs, in themselves or with their sculpted supports, are also of appreciable aesthetic value, including a very important exhibit known as the "Base of the Vicomagistri." This is the pedestal of a statue dedicated to the emperor Hadrian by the magistrates responsible for the territorial districts of five of the regiones into which Augustus had divided the city of Rome.

Temple of Veiovis

After a short flight of steps you encounter a mysterious *genius loci*. A colossal **cult statue of Veiovis**, found in the cell of the temple nearby, has been placed here. The statue, which has lost its head, was carved from a single block of marble, perhaps in the age of Sulla (1st century BC). The god is represented in a youthful, almost Apollonian, iconography, which we also find in some bronzes. Veiovis was an Italic deity, but we know little about his character, which some scholars believe to have been benign and others malignant, or his connection with Jove, with whom he is related by both his attributes (the lightning bolts and the goat) as well as the similarity of the name (Veiovis = adolescent Jove). Through two breaches in the walls, protected by glass, you can see the remains of the sanctuary dedicated to the god in the Republican period.

The temple was built between 196 and 192 BC, but later rebuilt, perhaps at the same time as the Tabularium, the rear perimeter of which was deliberately recessed to avoid encroaching on it. It is for this reason that the podium, at the left side and the rear, has remained intact. It is faced with slabs of travertine with elegant mouldings. A catwalk (which you reach from the room behind the passage on the Forum) enables you to look down on the building, which had a rectangular plan and faced west, towards the slopes of the Capitol. The cell of the temple is wider than it is deep. It has walls made

On page 150
Interior of the upper gallery of the Tabularium; in the foreground, the fragment of entablature from the Temple of Concord.

Dedication of Iovinus to the goddess Caelestis for the success of a journey. Musei Capitolini, Galleria Lapidaria, Rome.

Podium of the temple of Veiovis, detail of the rear.

of blocks of tuff and still has its travertine threshold. A short flight of steps leads down to the area of the ancient portico, with four columns preceded by a flight of steps rising on the long side and still containing an *ara* without any inscriptions. The temple also had an internal staircase (especially well preserved) which rose from the level of the Roman Forum to the upper floors of the Tabularium, but this access, through a doorway made of travertine, was later blocked by construction of the podium of the Temple of Vespasian.

The Tabularium

In the 1st century BC, on the hillside sloping down to the Forum, an imposing structure was built to house the ancient Roman Archives. It was

Cult statue of Veiovis, after recent restoration.

Constant Moyaux (1835–1911), reconstruction of west side of the Forum with the Tabularium. École Nationale Supérieure des Beaux-Arts, Paris.

Constant Moyaux (1835–1911), Palazzo Senatorio overlooking the Forum. École Nationale Supérieure des Beaux-Arts, Paris.

155

The frieze of the Temple
of Vespasian, recomposed
in the gallery of the Tabularium.

called the Tabularium because it preserved the bronze *tabulae* on which were engraved the laws and official acts.

Despite the importance of this architectural project, which caused an upheaval in the heart of the city as well as stabilising and buttressing the hillside, the literary sources are silent about the building. It was identified at the beginning of the 15th century through an inscription, since lost, that recorded its certification in 78 BC by the consul Lutatius Catulus. This was similar to the inscription that can still be read on a lintel in the passage of Via San Pietro in Carcere. Construction of the Tabularium can thus be related to the fire of 83 BC that ravaged the Temple of Capitoline Jupiter, restored under the same consul. Conjectural reconstruction of the building's original appearance has to be based exclusively on our interpretation of the surviving structures, which is made difficult by their continuous use through the centuries. In the Middles Ages they contained the "*salara* of the Capitol" (a deposit of salt, which corroded the walls), as well as kitchens, stables, the service areas of the Palazzo Senatorio, including the prison where defendants were held awaiting judgment and what is known as the "Sala del Boia" ("Room of the Executioner"). The layout of the ancient building is made more complicated by the loss of the upper levels, which were destroyed or merged into new volumes when Palazzo Senatorio was remodelled to fulfil its new administrative needs, involving the creation of offices, now clearly separate from the ancient spaces. Of these, the only one that can still be fully used today is the **gallery**, which provides a splendid view that stretches from the Coliseum to the Palatine, and was once a public passageway between the Capitol and the Arx. It was covered with pavilion vaults, of which the only one that remains is the last bay towards Via San Pietro in Carcere. It is set on a plinth—in concrete faced externally by enormous blocks of *pietra gabina* or red tuff laid alternately edge on and end on and now badly eroded by the wind—along which runs another, much smaller, gallery illuminated by rectangular windows. The upper loggia of the Doric order, with its eleven great arches (some of them only reopened in the late 19th century), must have formed a highly scenic backdrop to the Forum. Probably there was at least another floor above this, as suggested by the presence of some travertine capitals, which seem to have fallen from it, at the foot of the monument in this part of the Forum. Perhaps the second flight of steps mentioned at the Temple of Veiovis (and unfortunately badly preserved) led up to this level. From the gallery you can enter a parallel room which contains interesting remains (including a fine mosaic) of a building from the 2nd century BC, demolished to build the Tabularium. In the 18th century two sections of entablature from the temples below it were affixed to the walls of the airy gallery. One comes from the Temple of Concord, rebuilt by Tiberius (early 1st century AD), and has marble carvings of refined elegance; the fragment of the Temple of Vespasian and Tito (79 AD), with its characteristic chiaroscuro effects and the tactile qualities of the relief, has a frieze decorated with cult objects and sacrificial instruments. (*N.G.*)

The Imperial
Forums

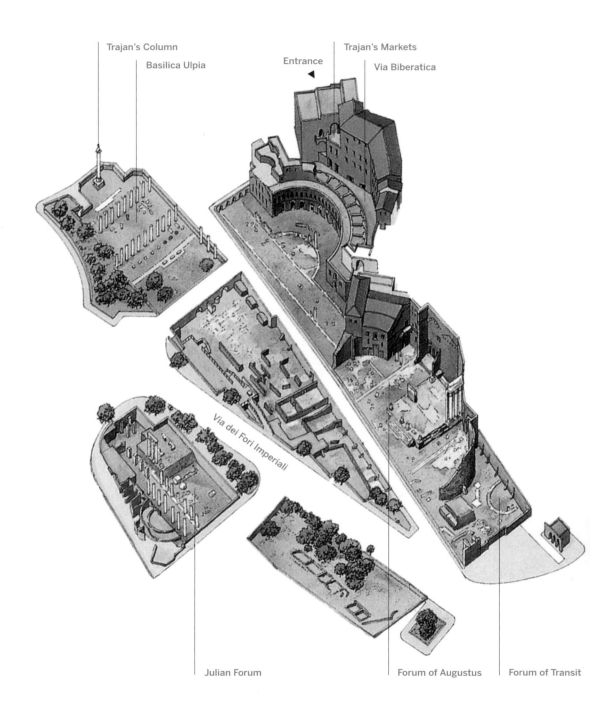

Trajan's Column

Basilica Ulpia

Entrance

Trajan's Markets

Via Biberatica

Via dei Fori Imperiali

Julian Forum

Forum of Augustus

Forum of Transit

Suggestions for a Visit

The Imperial Forums are today divided into different areas, separated by Via dei Fori Imperiali and Via Alessandrina, but linked by two underground passages. So we can follow a single route that takes in the old excavations and the new, starting from the Julian Forum and ending at Trajan's Column. This route excludes Trajan's Market and part of the Forum of Trajan, which have separate access from the Great Hall of the Market, where the Museum of the Imperial Forums has been set up. In presenting the site we are following the chronological order in which the separate Forums were built.

The letters between parentheses in the text refer to monuments identified in the plans of the different forums.

The Places of Consensus

Between the 2nd and 3rd centuries BC, the ancient Roman Forum of Republican times had become seriously inadequate to the needs of administration and display in a city that had grown into the capital of an immense Empire. Moreover, the ancient temples and various other buildings, erected at different times, hindered any attempt to replan the city. The need for new public spaces, together with the concentration of power in the hands of Julius Caesar, led to the construction of the first new Forum and eventually to a sequence of five Imperial Forums (the **Fora Imperatorum**) that progressively expanded the city's centre to the north-east, creating a new monumental urban hub in the valley between the Quirinal and the Capitol. The Julian Forum was followed in the span of little more than 150 years (from 46 BC to 113 AD) by the Forums of Augustus, Vespasian (the Temple of Peace), Domitian (the Forum of Nerva) and Trajan. The new Forums were planned on the principles of late Hellenistic architecture, organised coherently around a single axis, a design that was lacking in the layout of the Republican Forum. Finally they were linked to form an architectural unity, highly complex and very splendid, isolated from the rest of the city and laid out in five colonnaded squares that served the purposes of propaganda (by celebrating the emperors whose names they bore, and who had used the plunder from their victorious campaigns in their construction) as well as fulfilling a wide range of cultural, administrative, legal and cultural functions. Their isolation and their use for such "noble" purposes further distinguished them from the Republican Forum, which had some major streets running through it and was "tainted" by various forms of commerce. From ancient authors and archaeological excavations we learn that the Imperial Forums were built in areas that were largely occupied, already in Republican times, by housing, shops and markets (Caesar had to disburse exorbitant sums to purchase the land for his Forum); in some cases, however, they were new areas raised or levelled by extensive excavation to the detriment of the Capitol and Quirinal (as in the projects of Caesar, Domitian and Trajan). Today the appearance of the Forums, with only some of the ancient monuments still standing, is the result both of their progressive obliteration, spoliation and transformation in mediaeval and modern times, as well as their gradual rediscovery and study from as early as the 15th century. The Forums remained in use at least

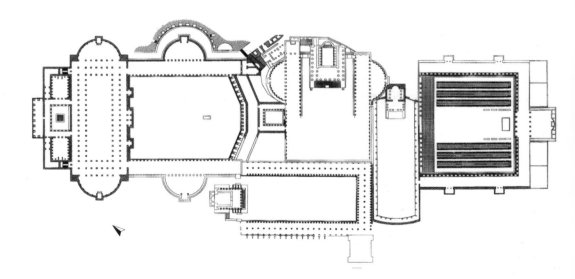

down to the end of the 5th century AD, then, given the size of the area they covered, each of the Forums and their buildings developed in separate ways. While the Forum of Trajan is frequently referred to in the early mediaeval texts, and the Forum of Nerva sometimes mentioned, the Forums of Peace and of Caesar were soon forgotten, followed by the Forum of Augustus. The ancient public spaces, now almost rural, were gradually occupied by churches and monasteries (in some cases as early as the 6th century, but mostly between the 10th and 11th). Then, in the Carolingian period, private houses began to appear, some of them quite luxurious, flanked by fortified residences (such as the towers called the Torre delle Milizie and the Torre dei Conti), signs that the urban space was being militarised. Permanent new urban development only appeared in the second half of the 16th century and entailed restoration of the network of sewers and construction of new residential districts (the Alexandrine quarter) and streets, which for the first time divided up the space of the ancient Forums into different areas. Trajan's Column, however, was fenced off, but there were still problems: in 1626 it was reported that there were "scandals and nuisances" committed in the area where the column stood, and that it had become a "cesspit that gives off a great stench." "Archaeological" digs in the area began as early as the 15th and 16th centuries, with surveys and drawings by humanists like Giuliano da Sangallo and Fra Giocondo, who observed an excavation in the Forum of Augustus in 1477. This period also marked the start of spoliation by "collectors" an alternative to the more common burning of the ancient marble to make lime. The first archaeological excavations were conducted by the Napoleonic government in the Basilica Ulpia (1812–14) and were continued by others as the century wore on, so giving a start to the study of the monuments and the first plan to improve the archaeological site (1911, Corrado Ricci), with permission for further excavations in the 1920s. These were true excavations and entailed demolition of the mediaeval and Renaissance buildings erected on the "ruins" from the imperial period, which were the sole

concern of the excavators. The massive, systematic destruction of all buildings erected since ancient times mainly took place, however, between 1931 and 1932 and was the fruit not of an archaeological policy, but of the Fascist State's need for publicity. The government wanted to make space for the Via dell'Impero, which now joins the Coliseum to Piazza Venezia, so permanently separating the archaeological areas of the Forums, reduced to a scenic backdrop to the regime's public ceremonies.

In more recent years, with the excavations of 1994 and those for the Holy Year in 2000, collaboration between the archaeological services of the City of Rome and the Italian state produced a project for the Imperial Forums that aimed to overcome, as far as possible, the divisions between the separate archaeological sites and, for the first time, to extend our scholarly knowledge of developments in the Middle Ages and modern times. This has made it possible to bring to light an extensive area of the Forums (covering some 15,000 square metres) and to provide a reliable reconstruction of its urban history from the Republican period to the Baroque, with a rich fund of new information concerning the ancient appearance of the Imperial Forums. In addition to the program of excavations, it has been created a museum in Trajan's Market to display the architectural and sculptural fragments from the Imperial Forums, where they are recomposed and related to their context. For this reason visitors to the excavations can understand the original functions and decorations of the monuments. Also on display are materials from the periods before and after the Forums, so providing a complete picture of the history of the area.

The Julian Forum

The Forum of Julius Caesar (Forum Iulium) was the first to be built. The purchase of the grounds was entrusted to Cicero; it began in 54 BC and proved very expensive (between 60 million and 100 million *sestertii*, but Caesar happened to be flush with booty from the Gallic wars). However the inauguration of the complex and the Temple of Venus Genetrix took place in 46 BC, while work was still under way, to celebrate Caesar's triumph over Gaul, Egypt and Africa. In 44 BC work began on rebuilding the Curia, which was moved to create an entrance on the new Forum and given the name of the Curia Iulia. The decision to build the new Forum near its Republican predecessor, though partly dictated by the practical need to combine two areas with similar functions, was probably not accidental. By building in the centre of the city,

Caesar

Caius Julius Caesar (100–44 BC) conquered Gaul and left an account of his campaigns in his *Commentarii*. He won the civil war against Pompey, becoming the master of Rome. He failed (perhaps because he never had the time) to find a solution to the political crisis of the Republic that had enabled him to come to power.
The greater the power and the honours he won, the greater the suspicion that surrounded his aims. His assassination left in doubt whether he, who was then a dictator, would have sought to reconcile the temptation to create a monarchy, apparent in the Julian Forum, with Republican legality, in which power was shared by an elite. (*M.C.*)

the patrician Caesar signalled his distance from his rival Pompey, who had chosen the Campus Martius for his building schemes.

Caesar excluded all forms of buying and selling from the new Forum, so distinguishing it from its Republican predecessor: it was a public space with purely civic functions. The dedication of the temple of the new Forum to Venus Genetrix, in fulfilment of a vow made before the battle of Pharsalus (48 BC), alluded to Caesar's own descent from the goddess, through the Iulii and Aeneas, the son of Venus and Anchises. In this way the new Forum was dominated by the temple of Caesar's familial goddess; while the Curia's new position brought this meeting-place of the Senate under his "protection" so revealing, topographically as in other ways, the new pecking order in Rome.

Portrait of Julius Caesar. Vatican Museums, Vatican City.

At least two statues of Caesar, now lost, were set up in the Forum. One, reflecting the use of war booty to defray the cost of the new Forum, represented him as *imperator*, since it was loricate, i.e. it showed him in armour. The other, by Lysippus, was ostensibly an equestrian statue of Alexander the Great mounted on Bucephalus, but the features were those of the Roman dictator, so stressing his similarity to the Macedonian sovereign, in which he was following the example of Pompey the Great. Various works of art formed part of the decoration of the Forum: paintings by Timomachus depicting Medea and Ajax, bought by Caesar for a large sum, collections of gemstones (*dactyliotechae*) and a golden statue of Cleopatra, which was dedicated, however, by Augustus as part of the plunder of war in 29 BC. The imposing

Julian Forum, the three columns of the Temple of Venus Genetrix.

Plan of the Julian Forum
reconstructed.

Julian Forum,
portico and *tabernae*.

Julian Forum, fragment
of coffering of the Temple
of Venus Genetrix.

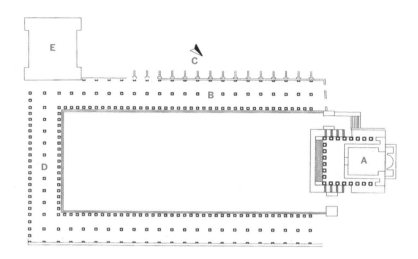

dimensions of the Forum, the statues of Caesar, the carefully staged ceremony of inauguration, the decision to receive the senators emphatically seated in front of the central intercolumniation of the Temple of Venus Genetrix, and the transfer of the Curia all reveal the ambiguity and even the anomaly of the dictator's new urban development. In a posthumous polemic with Pompey, he was now also behaving like a Hellenistic sovereign, using the city's new Forum as a private monument.

The present appearance of the Julian Forum has been affected by subsequent restoration. It was completed only under Augustus, but a radical over-

Sestertius of Trajan of 103–111 AD, showing the Temple of Venus Genetrix. Museo Nazionale Romano, Palazzo Massimo alle Terme, Rome.

haul of the complex was begun probably under Domitian and concluded by Trajan, with the rebuilding of the Temple of Venus Genetrix in 113 AD. Then Diocletian restored it a second time to make good the damage caused by a fire in 283 AD, and there were further alterations in the 4th century. The Forum was a large rectangular square, paved in travertine and surrounded on three sides by a double portico set on three steps, paved in white marble, which can still be seen, mainly dating from the tetrarchy. The Temple of Venus Genetrix (A) was placed at the back of the smaller side without a portico, without any attempt to make it dominate the space as was done in the later Forums.

The Inauguration of the Julian Forum
"He spent all the other days of the triumph according to tradition; on the last when the people had finished eating lunch, he entered the Forum that bore his name with shoes on his feet and crowned with flowers of all kinds. From there he was brought home accompanied by almost all the people and elephants bearing torches. He had built the Forum that bears his name, which is more beautiful than the Roman Forum; however he gave greater glory to this, so that it is called the Great Forum. In this way he built his Forum and the Temple of Venus, the progenitor of his family, which he immediately consecrated."
Cassio Dio, Roman History, *XLIII, 22*

Along the south-west side, adjoining the Roman Forum, you can still see numerous columns of the double arcade (B) and behind them the *tabernae* (market booths) from the first phase of the Forum (C). They are raised on two storeys in blocks of tuff and travertine and were used for public activities, such

as the Secretarium Senatus. On the south corner of the same side stands the **Curia Iulia**, visible in its late classical phase (E). It was probably supported by the passage leading to the Republican Forum and its presence may have been marked by an arch of honour no longer visible.

About half-way along the arcade was the passage that gave access to the Julian Forum from the **Clivus Argentarius**, the paved Roman street, still well preserved, that skirted the slopes of the Capitol. You descend to the Forum by a flight of travertine steps, flanked by a semicircular room with a long slab of masonry that suggests this must have been a large public latrine from the time of Trajan, set above the *tabernae* from the Julian period and equipped with running water to carry off the organic waste. At the end of the portico of the Forum, on the left of the Temple of Venus Genetrix, there began a second portico consisting of a double row of brick pillars set square and roofed with a double series of flanked cross-pieces: this is an enlargement under Trajan of the Forum, identified with the **Basilica Argentaria**, which was used, at least in the classical age, as a school, as suggested by the discovery of graffiti with caricatures and verses from the *Aeneid*. The short south-east side facing the temple (D), which backed onto another paved road, the Argiletum, also originally had a double portico, but later the middle line of columns was eliminated, as appears from the paving in coloured marble from the period of the tetrachy, which is still partly preserved. This seems to indicate the monumental transformation of this part of the arcade, which was probably given a new public function related to the Curia. The long north-east side, again with a double portico, is not visible because it is covered by Via dei Fori Imperiali.

The **Temple of Venus Genetrix**, of which the remains mostly date from the time of Trajan, was set on a high podium in *opus caementicium*, with access provided by two flights of steps at the sides, originally decorated with statues of the Appiadean nymphs. The building was a peripteral temple *sine postico* (meaning it had a colonnade on all sides except the rear) with eight columns of the Corinthian order in the façade and eight at the sides, of which three were raised. The rectangular cell had columns of *giallo antico* marble set against the walls and ended in an apse, in which was placed the cult statue of the goddess, the work of Arcesilaos. The architectural decoration of the temple was extremely lavish. The external entablature was decorated with a frieze of acanthus spirals, preserved on three raised columns, while the interior of the cell had a splendid frieze representing Erotes, of which few fragments remain. A carving of vine branches springing from a crater vase in Proconessian marble seems to have belonged to the entrance portal. The decorative program, dating from the time of Trajan, was thus intended to extol the role of Venus Genetrix, interpreted as the universal generative power of nature and so venerated with images of its vigour. This aspect of the cult of the goddess must have already occupied a central place in Caesar's program.

The Forum of Augustus

The Forum of Augustus (Forum Augusti) was dedicated in 2 BC, when Augustus received the title of *pater patriae*, but the Temple of Mars Ultor ("Mars the Avenger") had already been dedicated in 42 BC, before the battle of Philippi against Brutus and Cassius. Construction probably began after 27 BC and Augustus paid for it out of the wartime booty, purchasing the land from private citizens. However, he sought to avoid excessive use of forced purchase, with the result that his Forum was not as large as he could have wished. Behind his Forum was the Suburra, and it was set at right angles to the Julian Forum. Both Forums respected the principles of axis and symmetry and in appearance both were squares flanked with porticoes and

Portrait of Augustus of the "Actian type." Capitoline Museum, Rome.

Statue of Mars Ultor; copy of the Flavian period, from the Forum of Nerva. Capitoline Museum, Rome. It represented Mars loricate (armoured) and bearded, as *pater*, bringing out his "peaceful" role as the father of Romulus and *paredros* of Venus Genetrix.

with a temple on one of the shorter sides. Actually this effect was only apparent, because in reality the longer sides were each varied by two semicircular exedras, but these were concealed from anyone entering the Forum, being masked by the rectilinear colonnades of the porticoes.

The Forums a Good Place for Love
"Even the Forums (who would think it?) favour love;
The flame kindles even amid the din of the Forum
Where, below the marble Temple of Venus,
The Appidean nymphs whip the sky with water jets.
Often on this spot the jurist is seized by Love,
And he that is the guardian of others forgets to guard himself.
Eloquent as he is, often he lacks words:
The situation changes: now his own cause is to be decided.
From her temple nearby, Venus smiles on him;
He was an advocate and now he wants to be a client."
Ovid, The Art of Love, *I, 79–88*

The existence of four and not two **exedras** is a discovery made in recent excavations: the north-east area of the Forum of Augustus is actually known, including the temple and the arcade as far as the first of the two large exedras, but the excavation of the Forum of Trajan permitted the discovery of a second, slightly smaller, hemicycle on the north-west side of the Forum, destroyed to make room for Trajan's monument. For the sake of symmetry there must have been another hemicycle on the south-east side (not yet investigated), which in turn was demolished during construction of the Forum of Nerva. This discovery, besides showing that construction of the new Forums often entailed extensive changes to the more ancient ones and making the plan of the Trajan's Forum less innovative, since it is also varied by two exedras on each side, raises the problem of the layout of the south-west area of

Augustus

Caius Julius Caesar Octavian (63 BC–14 AD), Caesar's adopted son and heir, defeated Antony and Cleopatra at Actium in 31 BC and so put an end to the civil wars. Unlike Caesar he succeeded in solving the crisis of the political system, restoring order by means of the construction of a *principatus*, while giving the impression he was restoring the Republic. 27 BC, when Octavian took the name of Augustus, was the decisive moment in the birth of the new regime. In his Forum the *princeps* avoided repeating Caesar's mistakes and rejected all temptation to establish a monarchy, presenting himself as the providential culmination of the history of the Republic, as Virgil wrote in the *Aeneid*. In this way he also took the first step towards winning superhuman honours, which may already have been hinted at in the Forum by the chamber of the Colossus. (*M.C.*)

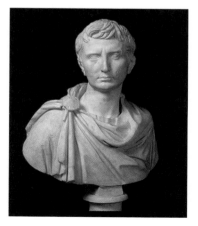

the Forum of Augustus, still unknown. The commonly accepted theory that the square was an open space has been opposed by another theory: that there was a **basilica**, with the two "new" open exedras on the short sides, set opposite the temple, as in many municipal and provincial Forums, which would thus have been based on the Forum of Augustus as an authoritative model. This reconstruction would help explain the numerous references to the activity of law courts in the Forum and perhaps also the impression of narrowness that it gave. Besides, at least in their decoration, there is plenty of evidence for the imitation of the Forum of Augustus in the provincial Forums, particularly in Spain.

The rear of the Forum was separated from the lower-class district of Suburra by a large **wall** in *opus quadratus* lined by bands of travertine, more than 30 metres high and still in existence, in which are set two entrances, one with three-arches (N) and the other with one (M, the so-called **Arco de' li Pantani**), at the side of the Temple of Mars Ultor (A). Flights of steps allowed access through them to the square below, subsequently emphasised by two **arches of honour** dedicated under Tiberius to Germanicus and Drusus Minor. The wall isolated the Forum from traffic and, being made of stone that was fireproof, also offered protection from fire. The square, of which only the north-east part can be seen, was surrounded by a portico raised on three steps (E and F), on which opened symmetrically the first two large exedras (C and D). Unlike their Hellenistic models (peristyles with the hemicycles of gymnasia and palaestra), they formed an independent covered space which probably housed cultural or judicial activities, a sign that the Forum had concrete functions and was not just used as a backdrop for displays of power.

The wall at the back of the exedras and porticoes was varied with niches framed between hemi-columns and had Corinthian capitals supporting an architrave with a frieze of vegetation, while the upper part of the portico was decorated with **Caryatids**, copies of the *Korai* of the Erechtheum in Athens alternating with *clipei* and, in the middle, heads of Jupiter Amnon. The subject, which combined the sophisticated classicism of the maidens (the Caryatids) with the chiaroscuro pathos of the deity, must have heightened the sacredness of the complex and also attests to work by craftsmen trained in very different traditions. The portico on the left of the temple also gave access to a room that was almost square (D), to all appearances a temple. It was dominated by the **Colossus**, set against the back wall. This was a statue about 12 metres high, of which only a few fragments and the imprint of the foot on its plinth now survive. In all probability it represented Augustus (or rather his Genius), as Martial informs us. On the walls, lined by pilasters with Corinthian capitals and richly decorated with both coloured marble and slabs painted to imitate marble, there seem to have been set two paintings of Alexander the Great by the Greek artist Apelles. The floor, well preserved, was also laid with coloured marbles, while a fine frieze of palmettes can still be seen along the north-west wall.

The centre of the square must have been occupied by a bronze statue of Augustus on a triumphal **chariot**, a choice of monument that differs significantly from the more "autocratic" equestrian statue of Caesar, with its allusion to Alexander the Great. Augustus also sought to evoke the parallel with Alexander, but in his Forum this theme remains in the background and becomes explicit perhaps only in the chamber of the Colossus. The intercolumniations of the exedras and arcade contained the honorary statues of the **Summi Viri**, the most eminent characters in the real and mythical history of Rome, each accompanied by an *elogium* commemorating his deeds. Of the statues and their inscriptions various fragments remain, some of exceptional quality, that show the choice of different types of statuary (some wearing the toga, some in armour, etc.), suited to the rank of the person honoured. The culmination of this program were the statues placed in the central niches of two exedras: on the left of the temple was placed the statue of Aeneas, surrounded

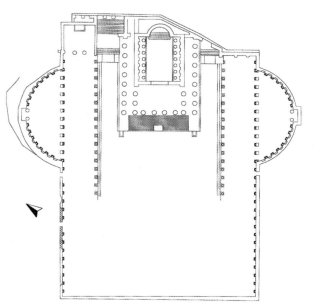

Reconstruction of plan
of the Forum of Augustus.

Plan of the excavated area
of the Forum of Augustus
(relief by M.L. Vitali,
Archeoprograma).

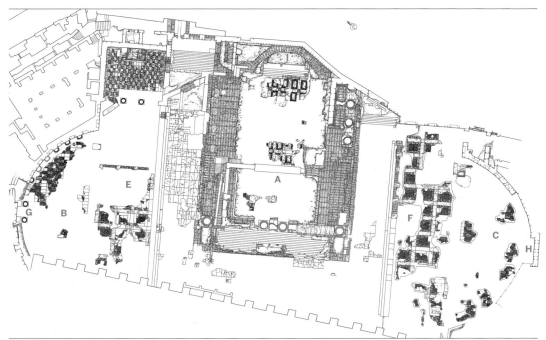

175

Forum of Augustus, columns
with Corinthian capitals
of the Temple of Mars Ultor.

Figured capital of the internal
order of the Temple of Mars
Ultor. The winged horses,
which seem almost to sprout
from the vegetation, with their
wings turning into leaves, are
those of Mars, the same that
appear in the apotheosis
of Romulus.

Forum of Augustus, the Temple
of Mars Ultor.

by the Iulii, his descendants (and hence the ancestors of Augustus). Aeneas was represented fleeing from Troy, holding Ascanius by the hand and carrying his father Anchises on his shoulders (G). On the right was Romulus, the son of Mars and founder of Rome (H). In this way Augustus related the history of the Republic to his own purposes, skilfully extolling the part played by his own *gens* and smoothing out all past conflicts in a vision of the glorious destiny of Rome.

The **Temple of Mars Ultor** (A), which backed onto the wall at the end of the Forum, encroached on the square at the top of its tall podium, with access provided by a central staircase where an altar was placed. The temple was a peripterum *sine postico* with eight columns in the façade and eight at the sides in Lunense marble. Only three still stand (L), surmounted with elegant Corinthian capitals in which the volutes really seem to support the abacuses. Behind the columns the wall of the cell is also preserved, defining the ambulatory decorated with a splendid coffered ceiling with rosettes in the middle and slabs of marble decorated with meanders. The cell originally had two rows of columns ranged close to the walls, which were enlivened by pilasters, their capitals decorated with two winged horses that seem almost to blossom from the vegetation. The building ended with a short flight of steps that led to the apse (I), in which stood a statue of Mars, known from various copies, and another of Venus. The apse also contained the standards of the Roman legions recovered from the Parthians by Augustus in 20 BC. The temple was closely related to war: here the Senate decided to wage wars or award a triumph, here the victorious generals laid down their triumphant standards, and from here the magistrates departed to their commands in the provinces. In this way the temple's original allusion to vengeance on the assassins of Caesar was extended to include the defeat of all Rome's enemies.

Pleasures of the Table

"Claudius was always ready to eat and drink at any time and place. One day, while he was sitting in judgment in the Forum of Augustus, entranced by the aroma of a banquet being prepared for the Salii in the nearby Temple of Mars, he at once left the courtroom, went up to where the priests were sitting and sat down to table with them."
Suetonius, Divo Claudio, 33, 1

The Forum of Augustus in the Early Middle Ages

Unfortunately little information has yet been extracted about the area of the Forum of Augustus, after the excavations in the Fascist period eliminated—without documenting—all traces of post-classical antiquity. As far as it has been possible to discover in the recent excavations and study of the sources and the materials found, we can say that in late antiquity also the Forum of Augustus did not greatly change in appearance and function. Deeper changes began to affect the whole area in the 6th century, until this Forum, perhaps rather before the others, became a sort of quarry: the fine materials of its buildings were stripped and re-used elsewhere. In this respect, the discovery of a previously unknown epigraph, carved on the inner side of one of the colossal drums of a column in the peristasis of the Temple of Mars Ultor, still lying on the ground, seems to suggest a later date for the chronology of the dismantling of this part of the Forum. The inscription is an attestation of ownership of the marble by an aristocrat named Decius, who can be identified in the sources as a consul in 486 or 546 AD; and since the position of the epigraph excludes the possibility of this inscription being made when the column was still standing, we can conclude that the spoliation of the structure of the temple took place in this period. The only building project we know of in the Forum of Augustus for the 9th and 10th centuries is the erection of the monastery and church of San Basilio on the podium of the Temple of Mars, recorded in the archival sources. (*M.C.G.*)

The Temple (Forum) of Peace

The official name of the complex built by Vespasian between 71 and 75 AD with the plunder from the Jewish war was the Temple of Peace (Templum Pacis), sometimes, but only in late sources, called the Forum of Peace (Forum Pacis). The building was destroyed by fire in 192 AD and rebuilt by Septimius Severus, only to be damaged again in the earthquake of 408 AD, by which time it may have been converted into a complex of booths and workshops. The Temple of Peace was almost unknown archaeologically until excavations for the recent Holy Year, though its appearance had been reconstructed on the basis of fragments of the *Forma Urbis Romae*. The excavations have now revealed an extensive part of the west corner and a large part of the central unpaved area.

The new complex was laid out on a site where the buildings had been destroyed in the fire of 64 AD, including the large **Macellum** (food market) dating from Republican times. In appearance it was a large quadrangular

Portrait of Vespasian. Museo Nazionale Romano, Palazzo Massimo alle Terme, Rome.

The Imperial Forums represented in the *Forma Urbis Romae*: visible are part of the Temple of Mars Ultor, of Minerva and of the Temple of Peace.

Vespasian

Vespasian (9–79 AD), of Sabine origins, a good general, became emperor and put an end to the civil wars that broke out in 69 AD after the suicide of Nero, so founding the Flavian dynasty. He remained emperor until 79 AD, adopting a policy of economic and administrative reorganization, remote from Nero's excesses and close to of Augustus's policy of acting in harmony with the Senate. His dedication of his Forum to Peace was an explicit allusion to the end of the civil war and the example of Augustus. (*M.C.*)

The *Forma Urbis Romae*

The *Forma Urbis Romae* was a monumental marble plan of Rome, based on the property records, ordered by Septimius Severus between 205 and 208 AD and fixed to the wall of a room in the Temple of Peace. Today it is kept in the church of Santi Cosma e Damiano. Numerous fragments have been recovered of the plan, which made it possible to reconstruct or to integrate our knowledge of the appearance of many of the city's buildings and particularly the Temple of Peace. The plan was orientated with the south at the top, and its scale was comprised between 1:260 and 1:270. It represents streets, public buildings (giving the names) and private houses, using conventional signs and indicating details like staircases, columns, etc. During the latest excavations a fragment of marble was found that also represented part of the Forum of Augustus; it has been interpreted as a working drawing or as a proof of the existence of a more ancient *Forma Urbis*. (*M.C.*)

179

Reconstruction of the plan
of the Templum Pacis.

Portrait of Domitian. Capitoline
Museum, Rome.

Portrait of Nerva. Museo
Nazionale Romano, Palazzo
Massimo alle Terme, Rome.

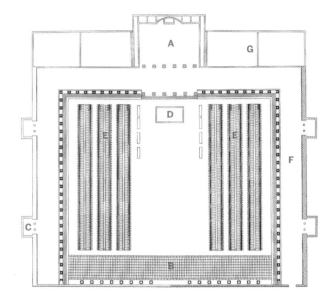

The Public Enjoyment of Works of Art

The use of the Imperial Forums for the exhibition
of art works was customary, but many of the
masterpieces in the Temple of Peace were
originally part of the decoration of the Domus
Aurea, which Nero had fill with works looted from
all over the Empire. Vespasian made them "public"
again (without, however, restoring them to their
places of origin) and his contemporary Pliny the
Elder praised his liberality in contrast
to the greed of Nero, who had enjoyed them
privately. The episode reveals the conflict between
the public presentation of art works (*publicatio*),
which enabled the community to use them to
embellish the city, and the private *luxuria* that
concealed them in the residences of collectors.
However, the latter provided the proper
conditions for their contemplation which, again
according to Pliny required solitude and quiet
(*in magno loci silentio*).
The question of the ownership and enjoyment
of what today we call cultural assets concerned
public opinion in Rome at least from the end of the
3rd century BC and was also used as a weapon in
the political struggle. Cato criticised the use
of statues of the gods as private furnishings;
a refined collector like Cicero praised the use
of works of art as an ornament of the city. An
explicit stand in favour of public ownership
of works of art was expressed in a speech
by Agrippa, in accord with the cultural policy
of Augustus. A connoisseur of art like Tiberius
had the *Apoxyomenos* of Lysippus removed
from the area before the baths of Agrippa
to his *cubiculum*, where he contemplated it in
solitude, but protests compelled him to restore
it to its original position. The problem was also
examined by the Roman jurists: a statue erected
in a public place could not be removed for any
reason, not even if it was still private property.
It was protected as an "ornament of the state";
its private owner did not lose his property in the
statue but only the power to dispose of it.
Moreover, at least from the 3rd century BC, Rome
had an official catalogue of the publicly owned
works of art, called the *Tabulae*, and from the
Augustan age there were also magistrates assigned
to look after them (the *curatores operum
locorumque publicorum*). (*M.C.*)

space, originally with the entrance set in the middle of0 the north-west side. This was changed by the construction of the Forum of Nerva, which then provided access to the building. On this side, towards the interior, there were free-standing columns in African marble with white marble Corinthian capitals set against the wall and a broad band of white marble paving, today partly visible (B), while the other three sides had a deep portico, made of columns of pink Egyptian granite with Corinthian capitals in white marble and raised on four steps (F). On this portico, on the north-east and south-west sides were also two quadrangular exedras, one of which is preserved under the tower called the **Torre dei Conti** (C). A small part of the south side-west of the portico has survived, with the steps giving access to it and the floor of *cocciopesto* (a technique in which terracotta fragments are mixed with lime), which dates from restoration in late antiquity.

The main side was on the south-east, opposite the entrance. In the middle it had an apsed quadrangular hall which was the actual chamber consecrated to the cult of Peace (A), the presence of which was marked by two rows of six taller columns, which must have supported the pediment of the temple but were aligned with the portico. The cult statue of Pax was in the apse, while there may have been an altar in front of the temple (D). At the sides were other rooms, known to us both from the *Forma Urbis* and archaeological study: part of the room to the south, towards the Basilica of Maxentius, has been preserved, because in the 6th century it was incorporated into the church of Santi Cosma e Damiano. This room was restored in the Severian period: the floor was laid with coloured marble, while the marble slabs of the *Forma Urbis* were fixed to the brick wall, where the brackets that held them can still be seen (G). The central part of the temple was not paved but contained a garden, through which ran six small channels (E) supplied by rills of water (*euripi*); along their sides were pots of flowers (Gallic roses). The function of the room probably also explains the height of the steps leading up to the portico.

The appearance of the Temple of Peace is reflected in later buildings from the reign of Hadrian, such as the Piazza d'Oro of Hadrian's Villa or Hadrian's Library in Athens, but there were also Hellenistic precedents and perhaps

Domitian and Nerva

Domitian (51–96 AD), son of Vespasian and brother to Titus, became emperor in 81 AD and remained in power till his assassination in 96 AD. He is a complex figure, who calls for reassessment. He was extolled by the court poets but condemned for his autocratic ambitions; he administered the Empire well, but clashed sharply with the Senate, whose opposition was finally fatal. Nerva, who succeed Domitian an advanced age and governed only three years (96–98 AD), was chosen by the divided senate: his principal merit is to have adopted Trajan, who became his heir. (*M.C.*)

some buildings in Rome in the earlier porticoes. Numerous **art works** were exhibited in the Temple of Peace. (Some bases from the Severian period with the signatures of Polycletes, Leocares and perhaps Praxtieles were recovered in earlier and recent excavations, while the sources mention sculptures such as the Galatians of Pergamum, the Scylla of Nichomacus and the Cow of Myron). They might also have been placed in the garden and along the *euripi*, but most must have been set in the porticoes and exedras. The building, which also contained the booty from the Jewish war (which we saw in one of the reliefs on the Arch of Titus), must have had a number of functions: it also contained a library and in late antiquity a medical school. Moreover, some scholars believe it was the headquarters of the *praefectus Urbis* and held administrative records and the property register, as suggested by the presence of the monumental *Forma Urbis Romae* engraved in marble.

The Forum of Nerva or Forum of Transit

The Forum of Nerva (Forum Nervae) was actually built by his predecessor Domitian, but inaugurated officially by Nerva in 97 AD. The name of Forum of Transit (Forum Transitorium) expresses its function of connecting the Roman Forum and the Suburra (conferring a monumental appearance on the ancient Via Argiletum), as well as the three existing Imperial Forums. The dedication of the temple to Minerva, patron goddess of Domitian, explains the name Forum of Pallas (Forum Palladium) used by Martial. Domitian's new development formed part of the restoration work that followed the fire of 80 AD in the Julian Forum and which probably also damaged the Forum of Trajan. Domitian built the new Forum in the narrow, elongated space between the Forums of Caesar, Augustus and Peace. Recent excavation has revealed under the Forum the remains of the **Macellum** and some late-Republican rooms belonging to private residences in the district (particularly noteworthy are the *ergastula*, the cells where slaves slept), as well as a phase of Neronian construction following the fire of 64 AD. Enormous foundations from the Flavian period (F), abandoned before 90–95 AD, show that at first it was planned to build the Temple of Minerva on the opposite side of the Forum, behind the **Basilica Aemilia**: it was later demolished and moved to its present position, perhaps in order to avoid overcrowding the square and obstructing the links between the separate Imperial Forums.

The north-east side is the only part that is now comprehensible and it has always been partly visible, as shown by the fact that the two surviving columns of the pseudoporticus were popularly called the *Colonnacce*. The **Temple of Minerva** (A), as usual, was placed in the centre of the smaller side, almost "shoehorned" into the space left by the exedra of the Forum of Augustus. The building was demolished in 1606 by Paul V and all that is visible are the founda-

The Chiavicone

During the papacy of Pius V, cardinal Bonelli, called "l'Alessandrino," had the system of sewers rebuilt to reclaim the area of the Forums, which had reverted to marsh. This enabled the district to become inhabitable again. The main sewer was the **Chiavicone**, built in the areaof the Forum of Nerva. This is an imposing work that has now been emptied to create a passage between the two sides of the Forum, passing under Via dei Fori Imperiali. (*M.C.*)

tions, the right side of the podium of the pronaos and the vault in *opus caementicium* that supported the cell, probably set in an apse. It stood on a tall *podium*, with six columns in the façade, and encroached on the square of the Forum only with its pronaos, which projected from the curvilinear walls bounding the Forum. Behind the temple can be seen the **horseshoe-shaped portico** with its apse, which had a row of pillars (B) in front of it. Its function was to conceal the back of the temple and provide access to the Forum from the Suburra through a trapezoidal covered chamber (C). This flanked the podium of the temple and was also connected with the adjacent Forum of Peace.

The lack of space hindered construction of the usual porticoes in the Forum, but to achieve the same appearance of a square surrounded by a portico it was decided to set the colonnade against the outer walls of the longer sides; the columns were then connected to the enclosing wall with projecting sections of architrave and so transformed in an avant-corps, as can be seen in the *Colonnacce*: the baroque rhythm this created varied the spaces and created the illusion it was a portico. The smaller side towards the Roman Forum was curved, so enabling it to be inserted between the Basilica Aemilia and the Julian Forum, and it had a monumental propylaeum that provided access from the Roman and Julian Forums (E); a second passage created a link with the Basilica Aemilia. In the Forum there must also have been a Temple of Janus, its position now unknown, apparently with four entrances that made it possible to look out at the four Forums ranged around the Forum of Transit.

Forum of Nerva, plan of phases of construction.

Forum of Nerva, details of the frieze on the *Colonnacce*: display of a woven cloth.

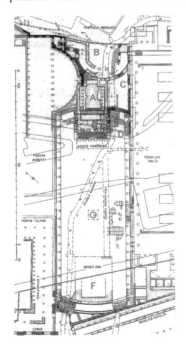

Provinciae and Nationes

In the decorative schemes of the Imperial Forums there are frequent personifications of the Provinces into which the Empire was divided or of the subject peoples (*Nationes*). The historian Velleius Paterculus enables us to reconstruct the presence of statues representing the *gentes* (particularly Hispania or Spain) in the Forum of Augustus; what is probably a statue of *Provincia* was recovered in the recent excavations of the Forum of Peace and Forum of Nerva. The widespread representation of allegorical images of *Nationes* and *Provinciae*, distinguished by their specific customs and attributes, testifies to the importance of this theme in imperial propaganda, which illustrated the extension of the Empire to all inhabited lands (the *Oikoumene*), as well as its ability to absorb and reconcile the vanquished. The armed images, like the one from the Forum of Nerva, showed the warlike qualities of the subject peoples, now prepared to defend the Empire. (*M.C.*)

The two **Colonnacce** (D) that have survived near the Temple of Minerva are in purple and white marble (*pavonazzetto*) with Corinthian capitals. They support an entablature in white marble decorated with a vegetable frieze rendered with marked chiaroscuro effects. Above them is a projecting frieze, decorated with scenes related to Minerva and female household tasks, like weaving, which the goddess had under her protection. The choice is unusual because it brought into the public sphere an iconography created for the private celebration of matronly virtues. A significant detail in the frieze is the admonitory example of the myth of Arachne, who challenged Minerva to a contest in the art of weaving and was punished by being turned into a spider (not represented). Above the architrave was an attic decorated with panels in relief: the only surviving element is a standing woman, wearing a helmet and with a shield on her left arm. She is the armed personification of a vanquished people, perhaps the Pirusti defeated by Augustus. This enables us to understand that there was a series of allegorical images of provinces and/or nations ranged above the intercolumniations of the pseudoporticus of this Forum. The presence of pivots shows that other colossal bronze statues were placed on the attic.

The insistence in the frieze on the theme of virtue and domestic work is bound up with Domitian's programs of moral reform. As *censor perpetuus*, he extolled chastity and punished adultery, making himself the guardian of the traditional virtues, like Minerva. The depiction of an example of divine punishment (Arachne) may have had a more pointed significance, since the Forum was probably used for inflicting capital punishment. All the same, the moralistic theme derived from Augustan models, which can also be observed in the personifications of the subject nations.

Forum of Nerva, south-west wall, the *Colonnacce*.

Forum of Nerva, the *Colonnacce*, armed personification of a vanquished people, probably the Dalmati Pirusti, known for their ferocity and skill in battle.

Aureus of Trajan issued between 112 and 114 AD depicting the Forum of Trajan. Museo Nazionale Romano, Palazzo Massimo alle Terme, Rome.

The Forum of Trajan

The Forum of Trajan (*Forum Traiani* or *Forum Ulpium*) was the last of the Imperial Forums to be built using booty won by the emperor in his Dacian campaigns, waged between 101 and 106 AD. The Forum was dedicated in 112 AD and Trajan's Column the following year. The construction of a new

Trajan

Trajan (53–117 AD) adopted a bellicose policy, not very different from that of Domitian; but unlike Domitian he was very skilful in maintaining excellent relations with the Senate, governing (98–117 AD) with the support of the army but respecting the senatorial prerogatives. Under Trajan the Roman Empire reached its greatest extension and the gold that flowed in from Dacia enabled Trajan to embark on grandiose monumental programs, though it did little to lighten the economic difficulties affecting Italy. In his Forum, Trajan glorified his new conquest, with extensive space devoted to images of the war, something that had never been done in the previous Forums.(*M.C.*)

Reconstruction of the plan
of the Forum of Trajan.

Trajan's Column behind
the remains of the Basilica Ulpia
in the Forum of Trajan.

Forum of Trajan, nave
of the Basilica Ulpia.

Forum, perhaps conceived earlier by Domitian, required an extension of the monumental area towards the Campus Martius and entailed cutting into the hilly outcroppings of the Capitol and Quirinal and levelling the ground on a colossal scale. The work, carried out by the architect Apollodorus of Damascus, also affected the Julian Forum and involved the sacrifice of an apse of the Forum of Augustus. This created a space that befitted a more highly articulated monument than the previous ones, with more striking dimensions and greater splendour, which also appeared in the extensive use of polychrome marble. Unlike the other Forums, the space assigned to the exaltation of the emperor was far greater: he was buried in the column and appeared in numerous statues. The figurative decorations on the column showcased his achievements in war: in the reliefs with arms, in the inscriptions with the names of the legions engaged in Dacia, and in the numerous statues of Dacian prisoners, while only the friezes of the architrave presented the customary sacred and pacific themes, which were derived, as a sign of continuity, from Augustan models. This kind of emphasis, more closely

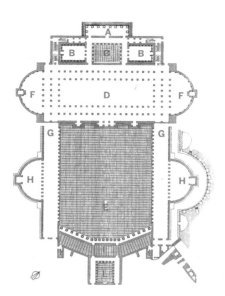

bound up with the present, hence clearer and less elitist, reveals the involvement of the whole imperial administration in the political discourse, in which the military element had great weight. It is highly significant that the galleries of honorary statues represented notables of the time and not eminent men of the past, as in the Forum of Augustus.

The recent excavations have completely revised the reconstruction of Trajan's Forum, above all in the areas that adjoined the Forum of Augustus and the Campus Martius. Probably there was a monumental entrance to the Forum erected in this area and not, as has been suggested, the Temple of the Deified Trajan, whose existence is known from inscriptions. The fragments of large columns in grey granite recovered (one is visible to the flank of the column) seem to belong to a monumental **pronaos** of the entrance with a Corinthian order, which formed the façade of the Forum (A). This gave access to a small courtyard with a portico with columns in *pavonazzetto* marble, where **Trajan's Column** stood, flanked by two buildings, now no longer visible. These are traditionally said to have housed the two **libraries** of the Forum mentioned in ancient sources (B). The interiors of the two chambers were paved with granite and columns in *pavonazzetto* marble, and there was an aedicule set in the end wall. Recent excavations have revealed the existence of flights of steps that gave access to at least

two upper floors, which might have offered a closer view of the friezes on the column. The poor lighting of the ground floors of the two buildings, which face onto a narrow courtyard dominated by imposing buildings, has led scholars to doubt if they could have been used as reading rooms. It has been suggested they served for the cult of the deified Trajan and his wife Plotina, founded by Hadrian. This would be in keeping with the rich decoration of the rooms and their plan, which is similar to the cell of a temple and had two aedicules on an axis with the Column, where the ashes of Trajan and Plotina were buried.

Between the courtyard of the Column and the great square of the Forum was the majestic **Basilica Ulpia**, used for judicial and administrative purposes (D), paved in coloured marbles and with two large apses (F) on its shorter sides (the south-west side, called *libertatis*, was used for freeing slaves). The interior of the basilica was veritable forest of columns, which must have made it hard for visitors to understand the organisation of the spaces. The building was divided into five concentric naves borne on grey granite columns (now erected again), in the lower order, and in *cipollino* marble in the upper. The two apses were lined with columns of *giallo antico* set against the walls. A frieze with Tauroctonian Victories probably decorated the architrave of the central nave while a second frieze of Gryphons paired with candlesticks may have been placed in the aedicules in the centre of the apses. Access to the basilica from the square was provided by three monumental entrances set in the façade. This consisted of a colonnade in *giallo antico* marble which supported the architrave, decorated with a frieze with Erotes, and of the attic, in which statues of Dacian prisoners in *pavonazzetto* marble alternated with panels decorated with arms.

The Emperor Constantius II Sees the Forum of Trajan for the First Time (357 AD)

"But when Constantius II reached the Forum of Trajan, a complex unique in the world, and, in our judgment, worthy the admiration of the gods, he stopped amazed, considering all around him those gigantic structures, which words cannot describe or mortal hands again build. So renouncing all hope of attempting anything of the kind, he said he wanted to imitate only Trajan's horse, set in the middle of the atrium, and with the emperor on its back. And prince Ormisda [...], standing beside him, replied with pleasing wit: 'First, emperor, command the construction of a stable like this, so that the horse you wish to have made can find as appropriate a setting as that we have before our eyes."
Ammianus Marcellinus, Histories, XVI, 10, 15–16

The great square (covering almost 9,000 square metres), originally paved with Lunense marble, had porticoes along its two longer sides (G). The columns in *pavonazzetto* with Corinthian capitals supported an architrave with a frieze of vegetation, while the attic was again decorated with statues of Dacians alternating with portrait busts set in *clipei*. Other statues of Dacians were set in the attic. In the middle of the portico were set two large semi-circular **exedras** (H), as in the Forum of Augustus. Today only the north-east exedra can be seen, in front of Trajan's Markets, which had its end wall decorated in pilasters in *giallo antico* and was separated from the portico by a row of pillars. Porticoes and exedras had floors decorated with coloured marbles, still partly visible. Inside the square, on the central axis but further towards the south-east boundary, have been discovered the foundations for a large travertine plinth that supported the bronze equestrian statue (E) of Trajan (**Equus Traini**), of colossal dimensions (over 10 metres high, including the base). It represented the emperor advancing with a lance in his right hand.

An unusual architectural ornament of a coffered soffit found in a recent excavation of Trajan's Forum.

Forum of Trajan, fragment
of a frieze with at the left
a Tauroctonian Victory
and at the right two Victories
garlanding a censer.

The new excavations have also altered our reconstruction of the south-east side of the square, which was closed off by a sort of continuous gallery (I). Its floor was paved with polychrome marbles and it had two lateral wings set at an angle and a central rectilinear gallery preceded by a colonnade, in *giallo antico* in the middle and *cipollino* at the sides, supporting an architrave that, at least on the oblique wings, projected as in the Forum of Nerva and was decorated with a frieze of Erotes and Gryphons. The gallery provided access to a quadrangular building (L), which may have been a temple, consisting of a courtyard with a portico paved with marbles (*cipollino* and *portasanta*), which partly survive. The porticoes were lined with columns in *cipollino* and supported an architrave decorated with the frieze of Gryphons and candlesticks. The structure terminated in an apse and here a monumental dedicatory inscription by Trajan has been found.

Trajan's Markets

Trajan's Markets are the conventional name of a series of buildings laid out on a number of levels along the lowest slopes of the Quirinal and abutting onto Trajan's Forum. The structure, dating from the reign of Trajan as shown by the seals on the tiles (but with Domitian precedents), should be seen as an integral part of the plan of the Forum, whose plan it follows exactly, and it was probably designed by the same architect, Apollodorus of Damascus. The Markets were a unified complex. In part they served to support and regularise the slopes of the hill behind the site and were used for a wide range of activities, probably administrative. This is borne out by an inscription found in the area of what is now the Giardino delle Milizie, which refers to the Severian restoration of Trajan's Forum by a *procurator fori Traiani*. The disposal of the waters was common to all the Markets and the building techniques are similar: the use of *opus caementicium* faced with brick in the elevations and with outdoor areas paved in *opus spicata* and flint tiles.

The Markets are divided into two parts by **Via Biberatica** (a name from late antiquity, of uncertain origin: it may be from *biber*, meaning "drink"), which is the pivot of the complex, though the functional relationships between the different buildings are not at all clear. The street (A), which had sidewalks in travertine and was closed to wheeled traffic, runs straight in its first stretch between the Large Chamber and the Small Hemicycle. Onto this opened a series of *tabernae*. Then it turns left and rises slightly, skirting the Large Hemicycle and the Central Block, until it is straddled by an arch that indicates the presence of an upper path between the Central Block and the present **Belvedere Terrace**. Finally it turns ninety degrees left again towards what is now the Salita del Grillo.

The upper part of the complex, at the top of the road, comprises the building known as the **Large Hall**, which was restored rather heavy-handedly in the thirties and features a large central room covered by a cross-vault (B). Onto this chamber, connected with Via Biberatica below, face three different storeys of rooms (the first has six booths on each side with their doors framed by travertine, while the two upper storeys are accessible by staircases). The function of the Large Chamber is unknown, but it seems to have been an independent building with an official function. This was followed by the **Central Block** (C), whose connection with the Large Chamber is modern. The building, refashioned in the Middle Ages, faces onto the sloping part of Via Biberatica, and is also laid out on three storeys, which communicate by means of staircases and have rather irregular floor plans. The first has a number of rooms and a semi-circular chamber covered by a semi-dome; the second is centred on an apsed room and communicates with the **Giardino delle Milizie**; the third has a plan similar to the second but is less refined. It is possible that the Central Block was an administrative building, perhaps the premises of the *procurator fori Divi Traiani*. The area of the Giardino delle Milizie is further up the hill and it had a practical function. It was occupied by a building from the reign of Trajan and traversed by a paved path, restored in the Severian period and known as the "Via della Torre." It can be reached by a flight of steps on Via Biberatica. Along the street are set the entrances to the Central Block and the Large Room. On top of the Roman building was later erected the Torre delle Milizie in at least three stages between the 12th and 13th centuries.

The lower part of the complex, below Via Biberatica, is a sort of open terrace set level with Trajan's Forum with the **Large Hemicycle** (D), which repeats the plan of the exedra of the Forum, from which it is divided by a paved street not open to traffic. This is the building with the most elegant decorations on the façade (concealed, however, from the Forum, because covered by the exedra), faced with terracotta and with a pleasing rhythm created by the arched windows on the second level, framed by brick pillars with travertine bases and capitals and surmounted by semi-circular, triangular and broken tympanums. A series of eleven frescoed rooms, with jambs and architraves in travertine and floors in mosaic, opens onto the street. The second level was based on a semi-annular corridor onto which opened other rooms. Finally the building had a third level, now destroyed, that opened onto Via Biberatica situated just above it on the hillside. At the extremities of the hemicycle are the two **end rooms**, covered with a spherical vault and with windows (E). The one at the north end is larger and has a masonry counter; the other is smaller and based on a Domitian building. Both were originally faced with marble slabs that suggests they had important functions. Behind the northern room and below Via Biberatica there are a series of interiors laid out on three floors and known as the **Small Hemicycle** from a room with a spherical vault that is apparently inaccessible. It has been interpreted as a cistern (F). (*M.C.*)

Plan of Trajan's Markets.

The rectilinear stretch of Via Biberatica lined with regular *tabernae*.

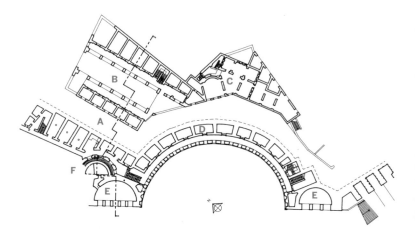

Trajan's Markets,
Large Hemicycle.

The slight incline
of Via Biberatica.

Trajan's Markets,
Great Chamber.

The Julian Forum
in the Middle Ages

Remains of the walls of one of the *domus terrinae* in the Julian Forum.

In late antiquity (4th–5th centuries), the complex of the Imperial Forums remained largely unchanged in their appearance and functions, except for some redevelopment, which was especially extensive in the Julian Forum. In the case of this Forum, too, the period of dereliction, or at least of deepest change, began in the 6th century, when debris and litter started to accumulate on the ancient levels. The crucial moment in the transformation of this Forum, like the rest of the complex of the Imperial Forums, came in the first half of the 9th century, when all its paving stones were taken up and the land reverted to cultivation, a clear sign of the process of "ruralisation" of the urban space, which was a feature of mediaeval towns.

The remains of very poor houses were uncovered here, dating from the 9th and 10th centuries: they had just one room and were built out of clay and scavenged materials. They were surrounded by open ground, where the inhabitants built the secondary structures like fireplaces and pits for keeping food. These humble homes—the sources call *domus terrinae*—of the early Middle Ages were concentrated in the more peripheral urban areas, such as the Julian Forum, because of the absence within it of any significant urban thoroughfare.

In the 11th century the irreversible reversion to swamp, which had meant this area was inhabited only by the poorest people because of the harsh living conditions, finally caused the settlement to be abandoned and from then on it was used only as farmland.

As with the other Imperial Forums, the swamp, the progressive covering of the ancient levels with landfills to reclaim the area and, starting from the 12th century, the massive spoliation of the outer walls eventually entirely obliterated the appearance and the memory of the Julian Forum. It became marginal to the built-up area, a situation which was only reversed when the city expanded again in the late 16th century. (*M.C.G.*)

Imperial Polychrome

The Forum of Augustus is the first in which it has proved possible to reconstruct the extensive use of coloured marbles in the decoration. They were brought here from the provinces and probably contained an allusion to the dominion of Rome (and Augustus) over those territories. The Temple of Mars Ultor, built in *opus caementicium*, was faced with travertine and Lunense marble, also used for the columns and entablatures, while the columns of the cell were in *pavonazzetto* (a purple and white marble), as were the pilasters in the chamber of the Colossus. The porticoes had *giallo antico* columns, while the exedras had demi-columns of *cipollino* marble in the first order, *giallo antico* in the second and entablatures of Lunense marble. In contrast with the square, which was paved with white Italian marble, different kinds of coloured marble were also used in the elevations, laid in a wide range of patterns, and in the floors of the interiors, laid in *opus sectile*. The same was done in all the Imperial Forums, namely in the exedras, porticoes, pronaos and cells of the temple, and the chamber of the Colossus. Pavements of different patterns thus defined the functions of spaces and guided the visitor. They displayed great skill in the use of colour to enrich the pure whiteness of Lunense marble (sometimes literally colouring it) and also served to signal the most prestigious areas, as seems to have been the case with the use of *pavonazzetto* only in the cell of the temple and the chamber of the Colossus. (*M.C.*)

Forum of Augustus, imprint of the left foot of the Colossus and floor of the hall in *giallo antico* and *pavonazzetto* marbles.

The Forum of Nerva
in the Early Middle Ages

Gold ring, discovered in one of the early mediaeval *domus* in the Forum of Nerva. The carved gemstone is an example of reuse that can be dated to the 3rd century AD.

One of the two *domus* from the Carolingian period in the Forum of Nerva.

After the period of late antiquity, the Forum of Nerva retained its ancient appearance longer than the others, because it remained an important point of transit between the Roman Forum and the Suburra, until in the sources of this period it was also called the Forum Transitorium. Then the ancient road that ran through it, the Argiletum, was repaved in the first half of the 9th century with a surface that could withstand the passage of carts; this made the road one of the busiest in mediaeval Rome. In the middle of the same century much of the area of the Imperial Forums was occupied by houses. In the Forum of Nerva, as shown by excavations in recent years, two large two-story houses (*domus*) were built at the side of the Argiletum: since they were built using durable materials and surrounded by outbuildings (storehouses, stables, etc.) and had facilities such as wells and latrines, certainly not common in the period, they must have been inhabited by the wealthier part of the population. Residences of this kind have also been found in the Roman Forum and Forum of Trajan, similarly ranged along the major thoroughfares, which suggests a feature of early mediaeval settlement, with the residences of the upper classes set on the main streets, while the rest of the population was huddled in secondary areas, as happened, for example, in the area of the Julian Forum. In the 11th century, the rich *domus* of the Forum were despoiled and replaced by much humbler forms of housing. Even though the Argiletus continued to be an important urban thoroughfare, the progressive rise in surface levels which affected the area during this period eventually obliterated the early mediaeval structures. It remained marginal until the urban development of the late 16th century. (*M.C.G.*)

Trajan's Column

Trajan's Column (C), 29.78 metres high, equal to 100 Roman feet (or 39.83 metres high including the base) rests on a quadrangular plinth decorated with reliefs of arms and eagles as acroterions. The shaft, encircled by a crown of laurel at the base, consists of eighteen drums of Lunense marble and terminates in a capital, which originally supported the bronze statue of Trajan, later replaced by St. Peter. The dedicatory inscription of the Senate seems to indicate that the height of the column was equal to the deepest excavations made to build the Forum. The Column was also the tomb of the emperor, who was thus buried like a hero, and of his wife Plotina. A door visible on the south-east side provided access to the inside of the Column and the sepulchral chamber, which contained a golden urn with the ashes of Trajan. It also leads to a spiral staircase, set in the marble and illuminated by small windows, that leads to the summit.

The figured frieze, carved in low-relief, winds twenty-three times round the shaft of the column, representing episodes from the Dacian wars. In this way it combines, in a new and original monument, the traditions of the honorary and funerary column and those of the triumphal painting and the historical relief. It contains some 200 metres of carvings, with 155 scenes, illustrating episodes of the two Dacian wars in chronological sequence, representing the principal events and also indicating numerous topographical details, such as rivers, bridges and towns. We should not, however, con-

Base of Trajan's Column with the door leading to the very sepulchral chamber, the dedicatory inscription supported by two Victories and panels decorated with arms.

Scene CIV, Trajan, in military garb, accompanied by two councillors and a lictor, speaks to the troops.

Scene CXLV, the Dacian king Decebalus, kneeling at the foot of a tree, now alone and pursued closely by Roman knights, cuts his throat with a curved dagger.

Scene LXXI, the Roman legionaries use a *testudo* formation to attack an enemy stronghold.

fuse the frieze with a true history of the war presented in images: the account is presented not just by pictures of military operations that really took place, but also the exemplary representation of scenes that are only apparently "authentic," alluding to implicit universal values. (For example the frequent scenes of sacrifice serve to show the emperor's devotion; those of woods being felled or the building of cities show Roman civilization in a barbaric land.) The frieze not only represents scenes of battles or sieges, but also of journeys or marches, work (the construction of towns, roads and camps), speeches and rewards given to the troops, acts of submission and sacrifices to the gods.

Trajan, omnipresent on the field, is the true protagonist, together with his army, but he is never represented fighting in the front line: this choice is significant because it forgoes a heroic image to present the figure of the "perfect" general, a tireless organiser who consults his officers, always takes the winning decisions and then rewards the troops who have carried out his plans. This was a model highly appreciated by the Senate, which commissioned the monument. For this reason Trajan is almost always shown in the company of one or two officials, a formula that isolates him and makes him easily recognisable, while also showing his vaunted familiarity with subordinates. The only antagonist is the Dacian king Decebalus, whose resistance ends in suicide, with his valour and that of his people

enhancing the glory of Trajan's victory. The reliefs also focus on the representation of the arms and armour of the Roman soldiers, their military tactics and the customs of the Dacians. They include harrowing details, like the depiction of the heads of decapitated enemies, or propaganda, like the torture of Roman soldiers by the Dacian women.

The spiral arrangement of the frieze has always aroused perplexity, given the difficulty of following the sequence of events and interpreting the scenes higher up. It is likely that, given the construction in sequence, this arrangement also favoured a vertical axis of reading, which contained the crucial scenes expressing the significance of the column. This is particularly true of the side that faces the Campus Martius, with the pronaos that gave access to the Forum: this represents the suicide of Decebalus and Victory writing on the shield, so separating the two Dacian wars, and one of the most curious scenes on the column, set on the second spiral and therefore clearly visible: a peasant falls from a mule under the eyes of Trajan and two officers. This is an *omen victoriae*, an omen of the victory, interpreted as favourable and accepted by the emperor. Its place near the beginning is not accidental because its auspicious significance extends to the whole campaign.

Some scholars have suggested dating the frieze to the reign of Hadrian, after Trajan's death; however images on coins seem to show the spiral decoration already existed when it was dedicated in 113 AD. (*M.C.*)

Scenes IX–X, Trajan, above, flanked by two councillors, sees a peasant fall off a mule.

Scene XLV, three Roman soldiers taken prisoner, naked and with their hands tied behind their backs, are tortured with torches by a group of Dacian women near a building. The women's cruelty is used here to describe an "alien" society and affirm Roman superiority.

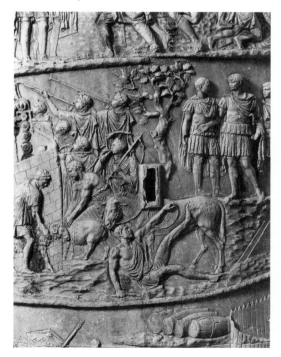

A "Masterly" Interpretation

In Trajan's Column the irregular sides of the decorations never project too sharply, so as to avoid breaking the architectural line, as happened with the other spiral column, that of Marcus Aurelius, where the supernatural enters the story. The background of the scenes is often lightly traced in; the figures are sometimes emphasised by a groove surrounding and isolating whole groups, which become elements of the composition, just like the trees, shields and walls. This is a notable innovation compared with Hellenistic art, though it seeks to preserve organic continuity and the full correspondence of the parts, as well as a markedly tactile quality, rich in shading, as in the art of Rhodes or Pergamum. The finish of the relief is not, however, smooth but rough: this means that the surface reflects a broken light and creates tonal contrasts that depend on the atmospheric conditions, affecting the perception of a cheek, a suit of armour, a standard. An important part, in this respect, must have been played by the polychrome decoration that scholars conjecture must have existed, but it has not been completely recreated by the restoration in 1981–88. In addition, the bas-relief surely also had metal elements, such as small spears and swords placed in the hands of the soldiers, which must have reflected the sunlight and identified scenes of battle.

Trajan's Column is the most original monument of all Roman art, the masterpiece of a great artist, perhaps Apollodorus himself, whom Ranuccio Bianchi Bandinelli, in an essay that has become famous, called the "Master of the Deeds of Trajan." Apollodorus was in charge of the general conception of the column, with a more fluid interpretation evident in the lower segments and with the carvings executed by a number of different artists, not masons but sculptors, capable of expressing styles of their own. They have been identified by Cinzia Conti thanks to close observation and a critical review of the sculptures of the various drums. To these artists, with their different training and backgrounds, we owe the column's formal variety, which emerges despite the unified tone that reflects the documentary character of Roman art in the treatment of the themes. The result is that there are few failures in the long narrative. So in contrast with the "master of the squat figures,"who has difficulty inventing

the positions of his often inaccurate images, we find the "master of the tapering legs" so-called for his elegant and slender figures; then there is the "master of the circular space," skilled at giving depth by the arrangement of his groups, often including the emperor, who participate chorally in the action; the "master engraver," who carves the Dacians as if in thin sheets of metal; the "master of parataxis," who arranged the episodes in a logical succession through parallel representations. All of them, however, revealed a poetic compassion for the vanquished, in some of the most deeply felt renderings of those who fall, crushed by horses or entangled and dying under the compact advance of the legions, the sorrowful exodus of whole peoples driven into exile, the suicide of the Dacians in their besiege strongholds. Here the inspiration of the foreigner Apollodorus emerges again: having created this new and authentic "Roman style," "he did not hesitate to condemn the romantic and morbid classicising aspirations of the great dilettante Hadrian, at the cost of putting an end to his artistic activity and, perhaps, to his own life" (Ranuccio Bianchi Bandinelli). (*N.G.*)

Cast of scene XXXII painted
under the supervision of
Ranuccio Bianchi Bandinelli
for the Italian State television
documentary *Io e... la Colonna
Traiana* (1971), in the TV series
produced by Cesare Brandi.

The Forum of Trajan
in the Middle Ages

Despite their scarcity, sources for the early mediaeval period are highly significant, because they describe the Forum of Trajan in the same way as the Imperial Forums, a sign that decay and dereliction could hardly have been conspicuous yet. Something, however, was beginning to change, since recent excavations have brought to light, in the chambers of the east portico, the remains of a lime kiln that can be dated to the end of the 7th or the early 8th century. This was a furnace used to extract lime by burning the marble, so abundant in the Forums, a clear sign of the spoliation of the ancient monuments that was to be a feature of the Imperial Forums for centuries. A radical change then must have come about in the 9th and 10th centuries: for this period there are no literary sources. Finally news of the Forum reappears in documents of the 11th century: here the square is described as almost entirely occupied by residences flanked by gardens and roads. So this is a fully urban landscape, that has no longer anything to do with the monumental space of the centuries of the Empire.

Also archaeological studies in recent years have shown that the first half of the 11th century was the crucial period in the transformation of the Imperial Forums. To this period is dated the restoration of the original marble paving in the Forum of Trajan. This shows that the function of the area as a public square survived at least down to the Carolingian period, thanks to the intervention of a civic authority that still sought to take care of the complex of the Forums. The subsequent removal of the paving and the temporary abandonment of the area should therefore be attributed, in all probability, to the fact that this authority was lacking.

To the beginning of the 10th century is dated the colossal project to reclaim this area, as a preliminary to its successive urban development: a project of such scope in this period must have been carried out by the city's government led by Alberic, the son of Marozia, and members of his *entourage*. This new residential district, which grew up some decades later than its counterparts in the Forums of Nerva and Caesar, had from the start the same urban character it was to retain until its demolition in 1932.

In the 13th and 14th centuries, a period of acute conflict in the Roman aristocracy, the northern part of this district, along the western slopes of the Quirinal, was partly altered by the construction of two of the major fortifications of the period. The towers known as the Torre dei Conti and the Torre delle Milizie, which still survive as evidence of that period, were castles built on top of existing monuments for reasons that are both structural and symbolic. The Torre dei Conti is in all probability the most ancient and almost certainly was built by Pope Innocent III (1198–1216) on a chamber in the eastern portico of the Forum of Peace, while the Torre delle Milizie dates from the mid-13th century and stands on Trajan's Markets . It may have been built by a member of the same family as the Torre dei Conti. At the same time, in the middle of the square, new buildings replaced the earlier ones of the 10th century: these were residences, mainly of the middle classes, with small gardens or vegetable plots at the rear, while on the major roads their façades were often embellished with porticoes and the characteristic projecting structures on the upper floor called *meniani*. The urban layout of this district did not undergo variations for about three centuries, until at the end of the 16th century Cardinal Bonelli, who came from Alessandria, extended the built-up area as far as the Basilica of Maxentius: since then the district was called "Alessandrino" and did not change in appearance until it was completely demolished in the Fascist period. (*M.C.G.*)

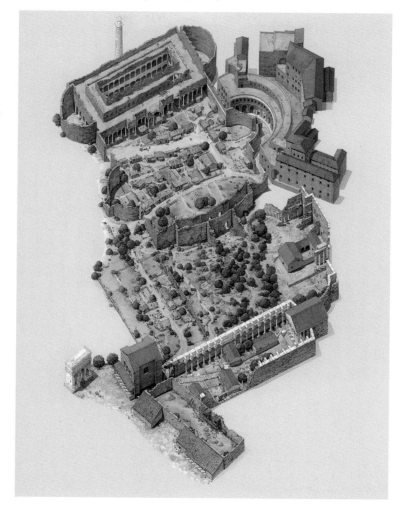

The Valley of the Coliseum

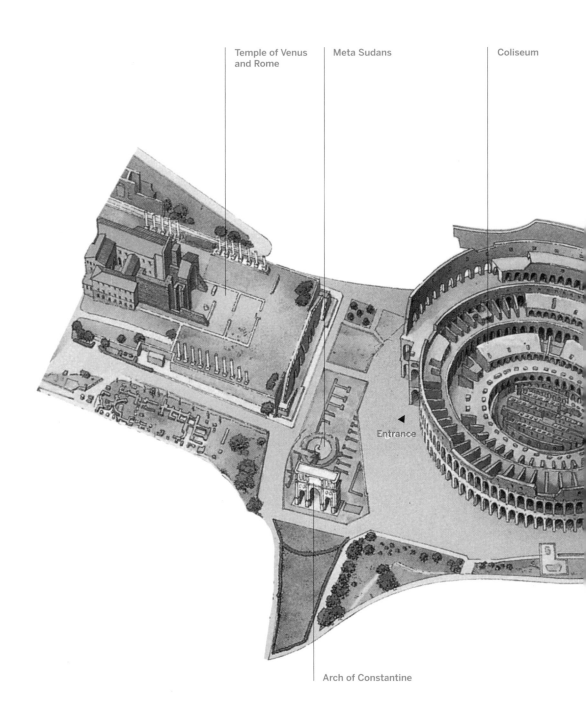

Temple of Venus
and Rome

Meta Sudans

Coliseum

Entrance

Arch of Constantine

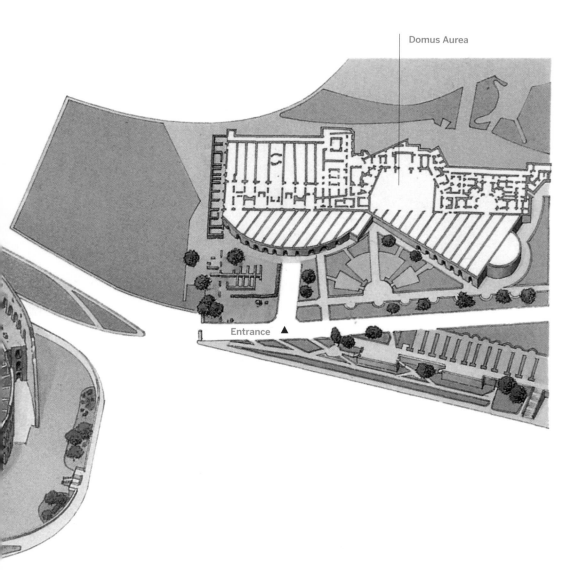

Domus Aurea

Entrance ▲

A Monument that Symbolises Rome

<u>Before the Coliseum.</u> The valley of the Coliseum is enclosed by a number of hills: the Palatine, Velia (levelled in the thirties to lay out Via dell'Impero), the Fagutal, the Oppian and the Caelian. In the past the valley was much narrower and deeper, surrounded by the rugged slopes of adjacent hills and crossed by streams that flowed down from them. Though the geomorphology of the area was not particularly suitable for human settlement, the valley had been inhabited since the origins of Rome (7th–6th centuries BC), when the populations who had settled on the hills for the sake of defence began to descend into the valley and shift the centre of their activities towards the Tiber.

Confirmation of the urban development of the valley in primitive times is found in the mythical traditions of Rome, in which the area appears as the north-eastern tip of the "Roma quadratus" said to have been founded by Romulus, and above all by the most recent excavations. On the north-east slopes of the Palatine, to the south of the Via Sacra, they have brought to light remains of a sacred area that was founded in the 6th century BC and continued to be active for centuries, down to the fire in 64 AD. Late in the 6th century BC the streams that flow through the area were channelled and the layout of the main roads, notably one connecting the valley with the site of the Circus Maximus, and then with the Tiber (today Via San Gregorio follows the same route). Public edifices and private residences were then built in the valley, until in the last centuries of the Republic and the early Imperial period it seems to have been one of the most populous districts of Rome, as well as one of the most important. This was because its western boundary was skirted by the route of the processions, as they came from the Circus Maximus, offered to generals who had been awarded a triumph. The first drastic setback to the development of the valley occurred in 64 AD, when the fire that destroyed half of Rome (and which some sources have attributed to Nero) razed the buildings in this district to the ground. At that time the emperor was building a palace for himself on the Palatine, which was also destroyed (the Domus Transitoria). He then used the valley and the neighbouring hills to create the largest imperial residence ever seen at that date in Rome, the Domus Aurea. In the centre of the valley, on a site then occupied by the Flavian Amphitheatre, Flavian built an artificial pool, supplied with water from the Temple of the Deified Claudius on the Caelian, transforming it into a monumental nymphaeum. On the south, west and north sides of the valley, the pool was surrounded with highly scenic porticos and terraces, of which some can still be seen today on the west side of the square of the Coliseum; to the east extends one of the great parks mentioned in the sources. On the Velia, the hill between the Palatine and the Esquiline, on a site then occupied by the temple of Venus and Rome, there stood the enormous vestibule of the entrance to the residence, where the ancient sources tell us stood a gigantic bronze statue of Nero, transformed by subsequent emperors into that of the god Apollo and finally the Sun.

Because of the death of the emperor in 68 AD and of the *damnatio memoriae* (a posthumous sentence that entailed the obliteration of all trace of his monuments), the buildings planned in the valley were never completed. The new dynasty in power, the Flavians, were responsible for the final transformation of the valley. They converted it from the site of an imperial residence into the district of public entertainments by building the amphitheatre and the buildings annexed to it.

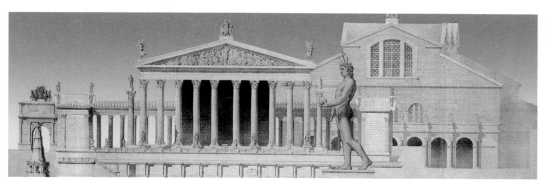

The Coliseum

The project of the Flavians responded to utilitarian and functional purposes, since the city still lacked a permanent amphitheatre, but it also had a political aim since, by restoring to the Roman people the spaces that Nero had requisitioned for the Domus Aurea and transforming them into a district assigned where public entertainments could be presented, Vespasian and his sons, Titus and Domitian, promoted a demagogic policy of winning support from the common people of the city for the new imperial house.

The construction of this enormous building took ten years: it was begun by Vespasian soon after his ascent to the throne and inaugurated by Titus in 80 AD with shows that lasted no less than a hundred days. So construction was rapid, partly thanks to the reuse of existing structures from Nero's building sites, and the cost was immense, but the Flavian dynasty was flush with riches from Titus's victory in the Jewish wars. When it was officially inaugurated, the works were not yet finished. It was Domitian who completed the last external orders and the hypogeum (underground level) which contained service facilities set below the arena.

All subsequent emperors until late antiquity took care to offer frequent public shows in the amphitheatre, a sign of the enormous popularity that the gladiatorial combats and the *venationes* (in which wild animals were hunted) had among the Romans. Well-known for his passion for the gladiatorial games, the emperor Commodus not only organised lavish shows but took part personally in the battles and wild beast hunts, calling himself a gladiator: it is a pity that we know from the ancient authors that these exhibitions were faked and he never really risked his life!

On page 214
L.-J. Duc, *Detail of the Elevation of the Coliseum, along its Major Axis*, 1830. École Nationale Supérieure des Beaux-Arts, Paris.

E.G. Coquart (1863), *Un Envoi de Rome*, École Nationale Supérieure des Beaux-Arts, Paris. From the left, the *Meta Sudans*, the Arch of Titus, the Temple of Venus and Rome and, finally, the Colossus of Nero, originally placed in the vestibule of the Domus Aurea.

View from the Coliseum of the western part of the valley. In the background the Arch of Constantine and in the foreground, interrupted by the circular structure of the *Meta Sudans*, some structures of the Domus Aurea.

Quite soon, under Pius Antoninus (138–161 AD), the first repairs became necessary following a fire. Through the centuries fires damaged the amphitheatre on various occasions because of the extensive use of timber in the structures (the planking of the arena, the scenic machinery in the hypogeum, the platforms on the upper order, etc.) and also the devastating effects of some fires on the stonework and the metal brackets that held the blocks in place. The fire that had the most devastating effect on the Coliseum broke out in 217 AD: the building was unserviceable for five years. In 222 it was again inaugurated but work went on for another twenty years: this explains why the structures of the amphitheatre preserved today do not date from the Flavian period but from the 3rd century AD.

The history of the Coliseum reveals its importance and centrality in the life of the Roman people and at the same time its vicissitudes parallel the history of Rome. Just as Rome, in the later 4th and 5th centuries, was damaged in sieges, pillaged by Visigoths and Vandals, and destroyed by earthquakes and fires, with the result that the city gradually became depopulated and impoverished, so the Coliseum after being plundered by the Visigoths under Alaric in 410 was seriously damaged and remained unused for years. Again restored under Honorius I and Theodosius II in the early 5th century, it was struck by earthquakes that weakened its structure and caused, with the ruins that accumulated in the hypogeum, the start of the gradual interment of its underground spaces.

As its structures decayed and there was increasing difficulty in keeping it in good repair, the city's ruling class and emperors, most of whom were now Christians, felt growing indifference or even aversion for the bloody gladiatorial shows. Though they still continued, they were no longer such a great attraction as in previous centuries. In 438 AD Valentinian III put an end to the gladiatorial shows, but the *venationes* continued till at least 523.

When these changes took place, it is easy to understand why the late 4th and early 5th century saw the start of the process of plundering and reusing the materials of the Coliseum, which was to continue for centuries and is the reason for its current appearance. For example, the innumerable gaps in the outer travertine façade are simply the holes made to remove the metal brackets that held the blocks together. The whole building suffered, particularly the interior and south side, to the point where the outer circle on the south side was eventually demolished, as can be seen today. The north side, however, was saved because it is stood on a major urban axis, the thoroughfare that ran from the Palatine, the seat of political power, and the city centre to the Lateran, the seat of the papacy. All through the Middle Ages and Renaissance, the Coliseum served as a quarry for building materials, with

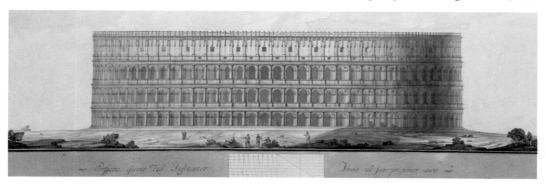

V. Brenna, *Outer Elevation of the Coliseum*, 1769–70. Victoria and Albert Museum, London.

Using the insight of the "stopped-image" of a simulated collapse, Raffaele Stern succeeded in freezing history, inaugurating the major period of restoration in Rome.

The valley of the Coliseum in a photograph from c. 1880.

even the popes helping themselves when they were building the basilica of St. Peter's. The Coliseum also served as a general container: in it people built themselves animal pens, small houses and craft workshops.

At the start of the 12th century, the noble family of the Frangipane, which at that time controlled the whole area from the Forum Boarium to the Palatine, built themselves a fortified residence in the eastern area of the amphitheatre. All trace of this, as of the other post-ancient and mediaeval structures, was obliterated by the 19th-century excavations. At the same time, over the centuries the monument had also gained an aura of sanctity from the memory of the martyrs stated by Christian sources to have been sent to their deaths in the Forum. This memory was made official by papal decree in the Holy Year of 1675. In 1720 the Stations of the Cross were installed in the arena and every year the pope performs the Via Crucis. At the same time, more frequent measures were taken to restore the ruined structure and curb spoliation. It was, however, only in the 19th century that

The golden light of a Roman sunset reveals the results of the careful restoration now under way, a long and decisive phase of the ambitious project of enhancement of the Coliseum at the dawn of the third millennium.

C. Silvester (1791–1830), *The Coliseum*. Tretyakov State Gallery, Moscow. A procession of hooded figures in the Coliseum.

The Myth of the Coliseum

In Middle Ages, more precisely in the 7th century, the sources first begin to apply the name Colysaeus to the Flavian Amphitheatre. This name, in all probability, referred not so much from the dimensions of the building but from the colossal statue erected by Nero which remained in the vicinity of the amphitheatre. This is further confirmation, together with what we find in the mediaeval sources, of the fact that by this period the memory of the original function of the building had long been lost and it was surrounded by the most varied legends. Some mediaeval guides speak of it, with that halo of mystery that surrounded pagan things, as the Temple of the Sun; others, remembering the words of the Christian writer Tertullian, described it with indignation and fear as a temple consecrated to all the devils. Only later did the studies of humanists like Poggio Bracciolini and Flavio Biondo recover the true function of the building and recognise it as the Flavian Amphitheatre of which the ancient sources speak. Though now a ruin and isolated from the centre of the city, which had shifted westward with the transfer of the seat of papal government to the Vatican in the 13th century, the Coliseum almost paradoxically began to take hold of the common awareness, its great size and centuries of history making it not only the symbol of the *Urbs Aeterna* but also, distorting its significance, till it became the symbol of the triumph of Christianity over its persecutors. Already in the 7th century the venerable Bede had prophesied: "As long as the Coliseum stands, Rome will stand, when the Coliseum falls, Rome will fall too, and when Rome falls the world will fall." (*M.C.G.*)

The Coliseum, a view of what remains today of the upper parts of the *cavea*.

One of the "Borghese mosaics" (early 4th century AD) depicting duels between gladiators. Galleria Borghese, Rome.

the first systematic excavations were conducted and the first major restoration completed. The hypogeal structures were finally brought to light, but with enormous excavations that unfortunately destroyed a great deal of information that would have been precious today. In 1805–07 Raffaele Stern built a brick spur to buttress the structure of the east perimeter, which was in danger of collapse, and Giuseppe Valadier did the same for the west side twenty years later. Subsequently, the interior of the Coliseum was also restored and at present the Archaeological Service in Rome is engaged in preserving and restoring the monument, as well as carrying out excavations and surveys to recover precise information about its history.

The outer ring of the Coliseum rises to almost 60 metres; the greater axis of the ellipse measures 188 metres and the smaller 156. The Coliseum was surrounded by an open area paved in travertine and bounded by big stone pillars, still visible on the north and east sides of the square. The outer ring of travertine (preserved only on the north side) is divided into four tiers: the first three consist of arches framed by Tuscanic demi-columns in the first tier, Ionic in the second and Corinthian in the third. The fourth tier is a blind attic divided

The Spectacles in the Coliseum

The amphitheatre was used for gladiatorial games (*munera*) and wild-beast hunts (*venationes*). The entertainments began early in the morning with the *venationes* and *damnationes ad bestias* (the execution of the criminals sentenced to death, who were torn by wild beasts); they continued through lunchtime with musical entertainments and then the afternoons concluded with the long-awaited combats between gladiators.

In this way the Roman public spent whole days at the amphitheatre, in hot weather and cold, watching spectacles that the modern sensibility considers atrocious and revolting. The magistrates vied with each other to organise events of this type and so ingratiate themselves with the people; the emperors themselves offered highly spectacular games and the strongest gladiators who proved most successful were favourites with the public, as well as with the Roman matrons! The origin of the gladiatorial combats can be traced to the archaic custom of human sacrifice to appease the spirits of the dead: it can therefore be understood how these fights became a sort of collective ritual associated with the funerals of important members of the community and gradually developed into a display of power and wealth by the aristocratic class.

This historical development can be traced quite clearly in the Oscan-Lucan regions, and for this reason scholars believe they must represent the geographical origin of the *munera* (while an Etruscan origin is favoured for the other kinds of spectacle). In Campania, moreover, the first permanent amphitheatres were built, with the one in Pompeii being among the most ancient, a sign of the success that these shows enjoyed.

In Rome the gladiatorial games long remained occasional events, though frequent, and it was only at a relatively late date that the need was felt for a building that would enable them to be presented: hence the Coliseum. But who were the protagonists of these games? Normally they were slaves, prisoners of war, prisoners sentenced to death, all people whose life counted for little in those times. And yet we know that free men also chose to become professional gladiators, certainly induced by the reputation it would give them and the rewards: the winners were awarded the palm and the crown of victory but also prizes in money. The vanquished met certain death, if the emperor, the *editor* (the magistrate that had organized the games), or the public refused to grant them mercy before the final blow. In their combats the gladiators were distinguished by their armour and techniques of fighting: there were the Thracian (*thraeces*), who had a helmet with high crest, a small round shield and a short curved sword; the *mirmillones*, with fish-shaped helmets, shield and dagger; the *retiarii* armed only with a metal shoulder guard, a net and a trident; the *secutores*, the opponents of the *retiarii*, armed with helmet, long shield, gambals and sword, and yet others of whom we know little. Also the *venationes* originated as shows presented for the people as displays of power and prestige: significantly the first time when exotic animals were presented at Rome was in 186 BC, to celebrate the triumph in the East of the general Fulvius Nobilior. Clearly fierce animals like lions and leopards made these spectacles even more fascinating in the eyes of the Romans; butthe stunning scenery (with natural settings, mythological panoramas, etc.) in which the hunting scenes were set in the arena always aroused new excitement. In late antiquity, for economic and religious reasons, the shows in the amphitheatre became steadily less lavish and bloody. Together with the decay of the structures of the Coliseum, there wasalso a slowly growing indifference to these entertainments, until an imperial decree in 438 abolished the gladiatorial games and, almost a century later, those involving animals. (*M.C.G.*)

The Coliseum, the tunnel known as "the passage of Commodus."

The Coliseum, detail of the stucco decoration on the vaults of the "passage of Commodus."

A figured Corinthian capital from the colonnade of the upper tier of seats (the *porticus in summa cavea*).

The Coliseum, the service passages under the arena.

On pages 226–27
The Coliseum, the interior of the building. In the centre, the underground chambers originally hidden by the floor of the arena.

by Corinthian pilasters into sections where square windows are set at regular intervals. Above the windows projects a series of corbels set under the holes in the upper cornice: they were used to embed poles that supported the great awning that was spread over the *cavea* to shade the spectators from the sun.

The spectators entered the amphitheatre through the arches on the ground floor, each of which was progressively numbered, which made it easier to direct the public to their seats. The entrances set on the shorter axis were not numbered because they were reserved for the authorities, while those on the longer axis were for the gladiators. The north entrance, marked by a small portico to stress its importance, gave access to the emperor's stand, set in the middle of the north side of the *cavea*. Today it is no longer visible because it was dismantled at an early date.

Once inside the spectators headed for their seats, following fixed routes that were differentiated depending on the area of the *cavea* to which they had been assigned. Admission was free for all, but the seats were rigidly assigned on the basis of social class and every Roman had a *tessera* or pass that showed the place he could occupy. The system of ramps, steps and passages not only enabled the public to be seated hierarchically on the tiers of seats, but it was also devised to enable the crowd to enter and leave rapidly.

The lowest area of the *cavea* (*ima cavea*) was reserved for the senators and their families; furnished not like the other seats areas (the restoration

of the eastern entrance completed in the thirties has been proved erroneous), but with proper seats made of stone. Since these places were the closest to the arena and so most dangerous, they were built on a tall podium surmounted by a safety railing. There is an inscription on the marble blocks reused from the parapet above the podium that has been partly reconstructed, so restoring the phrase carved by order of the urban prefect Flavius Paulus during a restoration project in the middle of the 5th century AD.

The inscriptions still present on the seats assigned to the senators record the names of those who occupied them: the names that have survived are of personages from the 4th–5th centuries AD, the last to have occupied the seats. The other *loca* (seats), that are distinguished with epigraphs reveal not the name of the individual but the fact that magistrates, colleges of priests, social classes and ethnic groups were permitted to sit there.

The second sector (*maenianum primum*) consisted of seats in marble reserved for representatives of the equestrian order. Further up were the places of the *plebs*, who occupied the third (*maenianum secundum*) and fourth sectors (*maenianum summum in ligneis*), naturally the most crowded. The last of these sectors, which corresponded to the external attic, was made of a series of wooden steps crowned with a colonnaded portico of which no trace remains: the capitals that survive can be seen today in the covered ambulatory on the second floor. Women also occupied the highest tier of seats, a sign of the meagre social distinction they enjoyed in Rome.

Finally, there was a highly complex system of collecting and channelling water from all parts of the edifice. Since it accommodated tens of thousands of people for days on end, it must have been equipped with the basic facilities, such as latrines, fountains, etc. In this respect, the capacity of the Coliseum is still debated by scholars. There are various theories, but judging by the ancient sources and measurements of the building, the most likely estimate is that it could seat almost sixty thousand people.

Today it is not easy to form an idea of what the interior of the Coliseum was like in ancient times. This is not only because the steps of the *cavea* are now missing, but also because of the underground structures which have been left visible. In reality, these hypogeal structures were hidden by the arena, made of wooden planking. The gladiators made their entry through gates set on the major axis: they entered from the Porta Triumphalis, to the west, and went out—usually as corpses—through the Porta Libitinaria to the east. The underground structures were essential to the functioning of the combats and the *venationes* or wild-beast hunts: they contained the animals and the machinery that raised to the level of the arena the complex scenery that formed the backdrop to the shows.

This sector of the amphitheatre was completed by Domitian: some of the sources record *naumachie* (naval battles) here organized by the Flavian emperors, but that must have been before construction of the underground level. At any rate, the structure that now exists is the result of the numerous attempts at restoration made through the centuries to repair damage done by fires and earthquakes.

The surveys carried out in recent years have made it possible to examine more closely two of the tunnels that led from the hypogeum under the arena to outside the building: the passage on the central axis continued eastward as far as the barracks of the gladiators (the Ludus Magnus) and to the south another gallery gave the emperor easy access to the stand of honour. The fact that this tunnel, built by Domitian or Trajan, was used by the emperors is deduced from the refinement of the decorations that remain (stucco, walls faced with marble, and painted plaster). The name it was given, "the passage of Commodus," grew out of the attempted assassination of this emperor in an underground passage of the Coliseum.

The Ludus Magnus and the Other Facilities in the Valley

Just east of the Coliseum are the remains of the largest barracks for gladiators in Rome: the Ludus Magnus. The remains revealed by the excavations completed between the 1930s and 1960s covered the northern part of the building, whose semi-elliptical shape suggests it was a small amphitheatre. The finding of a fragment of the Severian *Forma Urbis Romae* with the plan of the Ludus showed that there was a portico running round the *cavea*, onto which opened the cells of the gladiators. Here they would exercise, training every day according to a rigid system of discipline, but they were held in imprisonment. The Ludus Magnus, built by Domitian and restored by Trajan, is not the only barracks for gladiators who fought in the Coliseum. From the sources we know that there were three other buildings on the square with the same function: the Ludus Matutinus for the *venatores* (gladiators who specialised in wild beast hunts), the Ludus Dacicus and the Ludus Gallicus, which took their names from the place of origin of the gladiators who lived in the building (respectively Dacia and Gaul). There were also, most likely further north, the Castrates Misenatium, the barracks where the sailors of the fleet of Miseno who were in charge of raising and lowering the awning over the Coliseum lived. With its complex stage machinery, the Coliseum also needed other services in the neighbourhood: the Sanitarium where inju-

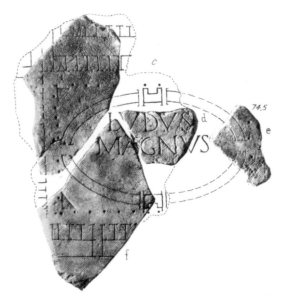

red gladiators received treatment, the Spoliarium, where their corpses were taken, the Armamentarium (arms storehouse), the Summum Choragium or store for the props and scene machinery.

The Arch of Constantine

The Arch of Constantine is the largest triumphal arch known. Placed significantly on the route of the triumphal processions, the monument was dedicated to Constantine by the Senate and people of Rome in 315 AD to commemorate his victory against his rival Maxentius at the Milvian Bridge and to celebrate the ten years of his reign (*Decennalia*).

In the Middle Ages the arch was incorporated into the stronghold of the Frangipane family; eventually, from the end of the 15th century, it was subjected to study and restoration. Studies of this monument continue today, dividing the archaeologists. The restoration carried out in the late eighties by the Archaeological Service of Rome provided an opportunity to closely examine the structures and technologies used in the construction of the arch, which proved to have been largely built out of materials taken from previous imperial monuments.

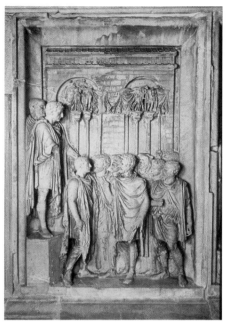

The Arch of Constantine,
south front.

The Arch of Constantine,
one of the reliefs of Marcus
Aurelius.

C. Rosselli, B. D'Antonio,
*The Punishment of Core,
Datan and Abiron*, 1842.
Sistine Chapel, Vatican City.

As a result, the traditional idea that the monument was the result of a coherent project belonging to the age of Constantine, which simply reused decorative elements from other buildings, has been opposed by another that holds that Constantine simply altered a whole existing arch, erected in the first half of the 2nd century AD in honour of Hadrian. To this structure, which had been preserved whole up to the cornice of the attic, Constantine's architects added the attic with the inscription and the other decorative reliefs, except for the tondi (roundels) of Hadrian already placed there.

Both these theories have energetic supporters and are based on valid arguments: all, however, are unanimous in attributing to the monument a remarkable historical importance, as a significant statement of Constantine's ideological propaganda. The model for this triumphal arch, which has three *fornices* (or passages) and is built out of marble blocks, was the Arch of Septimius Severus in the Roman Forum. The *fornices* are supported by four Corinthian columns in *giallo antico* marble reused from some other buildings (dating from the Antonine period: 138–161 AD). Set on tall plinths they are decorated with Victories, trophies, soldiers and prisoners. Flanking the central and side vaults are carvings of Victories with trophies, geniuses of the seasons and river deities, the typical iconography of honorary arches. Above the entablature, aligned with the columns, are statues of Dacians in *pavonazzetto* marble; they were taken from the Forum of Trajan or from some other monument erected in honour of this emperor, who was responsible for the conquest of Dacia. A low frieze, dating from the reign of Constantine, runs

The Arch of Constantine, view of Constantine's frieze and Hadrian's tondi over the smaller west *fornix* (passage).

right round the arch above the smaller vaults and at the same height on the shorter sides, decorated with the representation of salient episodes from the war between Constantine and Maxentius and the subsequent residence of the former in Rome. On the south front, this frieze represents the siege of Verona and the battle of the Milvian Bridge. In the upper register there are four tondi from the age of Hadrian, with the emperor and his retinue shown in scenes of hunting and sacrifices: the two on the west show the departure for a hunt and a sacrifice to Sylvanus, deity of the forests, and in the other two a bear hunt and a sacrifice to Diana. In the attic, at the sides of the large dedicatory inscription, are two pairs of panels from the period of Marcus Aurelius, with scenes of his victorious military campaigns against the peoples of Northern Europe. These reliefs were taken from a monument raised in honour of Marcus Aurelius, perhaps the arch recorded in the sources that stood on the *Clivus Argentarius* in the Roman Forum. The panels on the left depict the presentation of a barbarian leader and prisoners to the emperor; the pair on the right depict a speech of the sovereign to the troops and a scene of sacrifice in the military camp. On the shorter sides, the Constantinian frieze begins from the west with the first episode in order of time, the army's departure from Milan, while the east end depicts Constantine's triumphant entrance to Rome after the defeat of Maxentius. The tondi above the frieze imitate those from the period of Hadrian but date from the age of Constantine and represent symmetrically the Moon/Diana in her two-horsed chariot (*biga*) on the west side and the

The Arch of Constantine, Hadrian's tondo with the emperor sacrificing to Apollo, in a period photograph. Note that the head of Hadrian, normally bearded, has been replaced with a portrait of Constantine (photo Anderson).

Following pages
The Arch of Constantine, Trajan's panel with battle scene reused on the short eastern side of the attic.

Sun/Apollo in his *quadriga* (chariot drawn by four horses) rising from the sea on the east side. The reliefs in the attic are two of the four marbles taken from a frieze of Trajan with battle scenes, originally in the Forum of Trajan, or else from some other monument commemorating the conquest of Dacia. The decoration of the north front is symmetrical with that on the south: in Constantine's frieze the victorious emperor is shown addressing the crowd from the speaker's platform (*Rostrum*) in the Roman Forum and the distribution of largesse to the people, as a sign of munificence and liberality.

These two reliefs clearly reveal for the first time the distinctive style of 4th-century art which, beginning with the age of Constantine, influenced figurative culture in the West for centuries. Apart from the lack of formal elegance in this art, due in part to the mediocrity of the workshops where they were carved, there is a total absence of perspective and realism in the representation: the figures are presented only on two planes and the proportions of the characters in relation to each other and the architecture are not in the least realistic. The basis of this kind of art is, in fact, a truly symbolic function: that in which the hierarchy of the representation is of overriding importance. One need only observe the figure of the emperor, always at the centre of the scene, in a rigidly frontal position and unrealistically larger than the figures near him.

Immediately above of Constantinian frieze, in the tondi of Hadrian, there are, on the left, a scene of a boar hunt and a sacrifice to Apollo and on the right a lion hunt and a sacrifice to Hercules. In the attic are the four panels of Marcus Aurelius, representing respectively the arrival and departure of the emperor, the distribution of largesse to the people and a scene of clemency towards a barbarian leader brought into the presence of the emperor. In the central passage there are two other panels taken from the great frieze of Trajan: the one on the east represents the emperor's triumphant entrance to Rome (his victory symbolized by the winged deity that follows him) with the inscription *"Fundatori quietis"* ("to the founder of peace"); while to the west is a scene of battle with the inscription *"Liberatori Urbis"* ("to the liberator of Rome").

As can be seen from this short description, this arch is decorated with numerous scenes, which differ by subject, period and style. And yet, despite their variety, there is clearly a definite program underlying the choice and combination of these images. Their iconographic purpose was to communicate the imperial message as effectively as possible. In this monument Constantine chose not to be celebrated just as the vanquisher of his rival Maxentius, but to legitimize his power by comparing himself, in an ideal continuity, to the great emperors of the 2nd century: Trajan, Marcus Aurelius and Hadrian were distinguished for their good government, harmonious relations with the Senate, while Trajan and Marcus Aurelius were also noted for their conquests. The combination of scenes of war on the south front with scenes of peace and civil life on the north was meant to accompany the triumphal procession which moved from the exterior (south) to the interior (north) of the city, presenting Constantine as the bringer of peace and legitimizing his campaign against Maxentius as if it had been a war of conquest. On the other hand, the scenes of the emperor hunting and of the Sun and Moon expressed the eternity of the imperial power and of Rome, themes very dear to Hadrian and to Constantine himself, who in this way ascribed a cosmic significance to his victory.

Every scene in which the emperor appeared was also specially chosen because it represented one of the fundamental virtues of the good sovereign: *clementia* towards the vanquished, *liberalitas* to his people, *pietas* to the gods, and so on. This virtual continuity with his predecessors, one might say his identification with them, was also achieved by the transformation of their faces into portraits of Constantine. So the reuse of these materials (*spolia*) was done not so much for the sake of economy (though this practice had long existed in Rome because of the difficulty of obtaining building materials), as for precise propaganda purposes.

The *Meta Sudans*

Close by the Arch of Constantine excavations are bringing to light what remains of the circular base of a monumental fountain called the *Meta Sudans*. Erected under Domitian, we know from depictions on contemporary coins that it consisted of two superimposed elements: a cylinder decorated with niches and on top of this a cone surmounted, in turn, by a spherical (or flower-shaped) coping. The central cone-shaped element, which is recorded in eight hundred photographs dating from the late 19th century, was demolished in the Fascist period. It took its name from its resemblance to the pillar (*meta*) that marked the turning point in the circus, hence its name, and *sudans* for the water that gushed out of it. Its position in the topography of Rome was highly significant: it stood at the crossing of four or five of Augustus's *regiones* and at the intersection of four very ancient roads; it was also set on the same axis as the route of the triumphal processions that returned from the Circus Maximus along what is now Via San Gregorio, and when they drew level with the fountain turned into the Via Sacra. The symbolic importance of this monument agrees with the theory that sees this zone as one of the vertices of the Romulean city. If this is so, then the fountain must have been the monumental record of the mythical boundary

View of the Coliseum with the Meta Sudans and Arch of Constantine in a photograph from 1860–70, before the monumental fountain was demolished in the 1930s to make way for the Fascist Via dei Trionfi. Museo di Roma. Archivio Fotografico Comunale.

stone. The sources also record that the house that was the birthplace of Augustus stood in this part of the valley: the conical shape, so original for a fountain, has therefore been explained by scholars as an allusion to the *betyl*, the aniconic symbol of Apollo, the god whom Augustus recognised as his patron.

The Temple of Venus and Rome

On the imposing artificial base that still appears on the west side of the valley of the Coliseum are the remains of the largest temple Rome ever had: the temple dedicated to the Eternal City and to the goddess Venus, the mother of Aeneas, the founder of the city. The building was erected on the slopes of the Velian hill, with work beginning in 121 AD by order of Hadrian to his own design. Hadrian was in fact a many-sided character: he had a very broad culture, literary and artistic but also technical, he was soldier, poet, architect and engineer; his philhellenism affected a whole period of art, culture and Roman life. The temple was built on a site previously occupied by the vestibule of the Domus Aurea, retaining its orientation and partly reusing its foundations. Before it could be built workmen had to move the colossal statue of Nero, the biggest bronze statue ever made in the ancient world (at least 35 metres high Pliny says). The sources state it was moved to a new base built closer to the amphitheatre, where it was taken in by employing a cart drawn by twenty-four elephants. The remains of this base were finally demolished in the 1930s to make way for Via dell'Impero. This temple, with its Hellenistic forms, reflecting the emperor's own tastes, stood at the centre of a large artificial podium. This was supported on the long sides by a double portico of columns in grey granite, at the centre of which were set two propylaea, while on the short sides it was connected by flights of steps to the square of the Coliseum and the Forum. The columns visible today were raised during restoration in the thirties. The actual temple is dipteral, since it has two cells oriented in opposite directions (one for each deity venerated), and preceded by a pronaos (or vestibule). Of the peristyle of Corinthian columns nothing remains, and of the cell facing the Coliseum (dedicated to Venus) only the apse; however the cell on the west side is far better preserved, having been incorporated at quite an early date into the former convent of Santa Romana Francesca. However what we see today does not date from the original temple built under Hadrian (perhaps with the exception of some parts of the paving of the cells) but to extensive restoration under Maxentius in 307 AD, following a fire that destroyed the whole central part of the Forum and so enabled him to start construction of the large basilica that bears his name. To this restoration we owe the apsed cells made of brick and covered with coffered vaulting, the stucco decorations of the coffering, the columns porphyry ranged along the walls and the floor laid with marble slabs still quite visible inside the former convent. This suggests the great importance still surrounding this shrine dedicated to the religion of Rome two centuries later. (*M.C.G.*)

The temple of Venus and Rome on the high podium, seen from the Coliseum.

The temple of Venus and Rome, the west cell absorbed into the convent of Santa Francesca Romana.

The Domus Aurea

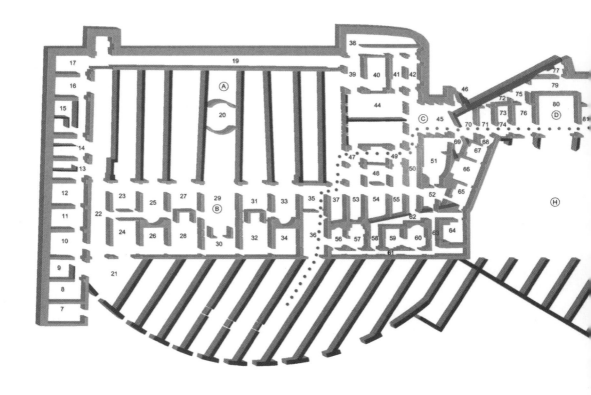

Suggestions for a Visit

The entrance is on Via della Domus Aurea, which climbs up the Oppian Hill from the square of the Coliseum. Because of the numbers of tourists and the need to protect the building, especially the delicate microclimate inside, access is regulated and bookings are required. Visits are organized in groups of 25 people who have a guided tour (220 metres, 32 rooms), which lasts about 45 minutes. It is important to bear in mind that the temperature underground in summer is about 12 degrees, falling to 4 degrees in winter.

Trajan's Walls

Walls of the Horrea Built by Claudius

Visitors' Route

A. Peristyle
B. Room with the Vault
   of the Little Owls
C. Nymphaeum of Ulysses
   and Polyphemus
D. Room of the Gilded Vaults
E. Room of Achilles at Skyros
F. Octagonal Room
G. Room of Hector
   and Andromache
H. Courtyard

Legend, History, Fortune

Nero's Golden Dream: the Architecture, the Decorations.

"Everything in it was covered gold": with this effective formula Suetonius summed up a fantasia that came true. In building the Domus Aurea, Nero had taken Seneca at his word. In the *Apocolocynthosis* the philosopher celebrated the coming of the emperor, the dawn of the new century of gold, and has Apollo say: "The radiant Sun contemplates the universe. So Caesar appears, and so Rome will contemplate Nero," in the colossus over 30 metres high, made of forged bronze gilded by the sculptor Zenodoros, which rose proudly at the entrance to his fabulous palace. Nero was not the first emperor faced with the problem of creating an official residence. A political necessity first before that of vanity or passion for the luxury: in Rome arrived in fact foreign monarchs, allies or subject, many of them accustomed to the style of life of the Hellenistic and Oriental kingdoms. These princely models inspired the ideology of the project, which included pavilions immersed in gardens populated with all sorts of rural delights and fostering the communion between man and nature. It is said that Nero had succeeded in bringing the countryside into the heart of the city and that his forests of wild beasts evoked the "paradises" of the Persian kings. The same ideal was later embodied in Hadrian's Villa, and then returned to favour with the Renaissance and the Baroque until it to bred unfortunately substantial misunderstandings in Michael Jackson's Neverlands Ranch. But predecessors and successors cautiously avoided the excesses of megalomania, "merely" occupying the Palatine, till the term *palatium* came to signify, as in English "palace" and other derivatives in almost all European languages, a princely or aristocratic residence. Augustus was satisfied with a simple residence, though of extreme refinement close by that of Livia, so that the first true palace was the Domus Tiberiana, the seat of the Julian-Claudian line. After the fire of 64 AD, Nero decided to transform its previous design to achieve an unusual degree of magnificence, taking advantage of the large space left in the centre of Rome by the districts the fire had rased and ordering the expropriation and demolition of whole areas spared by the flames (the luxurious residences of senators, all the better if they were political opponents, together with the poor houses of the common people and even temples). The magnificence and extension of the Domus Aurea now became legendary, like its creators recorded by Tacitus: Severus and Celeres, *magistri* and *machinatores*, architects and engineers capable of conceiving original variations while drawing inspiration from the great maritime villas of the Gulf of Naples, naturally without neglecting the structural and technical aspects; and there were some who see their names as containing an allusion to the responsibility and speed with which the work was conducted, so that already in 66 AD the emperor was settled into his new residence.

A First-Hand Description

The Roman scholar and biographer Suetonius saw the Domus Aurea and evoked it expressively in his Life of Nero: "The vestibule of the house was so big it contained a colossal statue 120 feet high, the image of Nero; and it was so extensive that it had three colonnades a mile long. There was a lake too, in fact a sea, surrounded with buildings as big as cities. Behind it were villas with fields, vineyards and pastures, woods filled with all kinds of wild and domestic animals. In the rest of the house everything was coated with gold and adorned with gems and shells. The dining-rooms had fretted ceilings made of ivory, with panels that turned and shed flowers and perfumes on those below. The main banquet hall was circular and constantly revolved day and night, like the heavens. He had baths supplied with sea water and sulphur water. When Nero dedicated the house on the completion of work, he appeared satisfied, and said at last he was beginning to be housed like a man."

Roma domus fiet: Veios migrate Quirites / si non et Veios occupat ista domus! "Rome is now one huge house: Romans, migrate to the town Veio! ... that is, if that house hasn't sprawled all the way to Veio!" This famous satire expresses the popular resentment at the seizure of a large part of the south-east part of the city, an area of over 80 hectares, almost twice the surface area of the present Vatican City.

The buildings laid out between the Palatine and Velian hills occupied the Oppian Hill as far as the Esquiline and to the Caelian, where the Temple of the Deified Claudius was converted into a monumental nymphaeum. Some of the structures and pictorial decorations of the building on the Palatine—called the Domus Transitoria because it joined the imperial palace on the Palatine to the emperor gardens on the Esquiline—were brought to light during excavations of the Domus Augustana, the residence of Domitian built by the architect Rabirius, who preferred to incorporate these remains rather than demolish them. Extensive remains of the Domus Aurea were also recovered in the area of the Temple of Venus and Rome, near the Via Sacra, where the Colossus stood in its grandiose *vestibulum*. Other remains appeared during recent excavations in the area of the *Meta Sudans*, in front of the Coliseum, where in the lowest part of the valley there was once the *stagnum*, an artificial lake, its shores surrounded by gardens and woods, porticoes and terraces, recreating the scenery of a little harbour.

Nero, the Architect of Excess

"Greedy for the impossible." Tacitus took just two words (*incredibilium concuptor*) to express the senatorial opposition's harsh opinion even of the emperor's building policy, considered the bankrupt expression of a visionary temperament. The historian Andrea Giardina has pointed out that the construction of immense and splendid buildings, of daring works that prevail over man and nature, were part of the "heroic" model that Nero desired to embody. Giardina observes that in the Domus Aurea, "Nero took advantage of the destruction of the city to build a residence which stunned people not so much by the gems and gold, already widely used as an expression of luxury and by this time quite banal, as by the fields and pools, with—in imitation of wild nature—here forests, there open spaces and panoramic views. In their design, Severus and Celeres had the intelligence and boldness to dare to create through their art what nature had denied, and squander the resources of the prince."

Some decades earlier Caesar, with the *lex de Urbe augenda*, had proposed to move the course of the Tiber to include extensive new areas in Rome's urban fabric of the capital. Now Nero took up an ambitious plan of the enterprising dictator's for the excavation of an artificial channel navigable for 250 kilometres from Lake Avernus near Cumae to the mouth of the Tiber, so that the cargoes of Egyptian wheat could be brought up to the city in boats of shallower draught. This would have avoided the frequent disasters that happened along the coasts and in the port of Ostium itself, which he wanted to include within the city walls by bringing the sea inside the city. An even more superhuman undertaking was the idea of cutting through the Isthmus of Corinth, after eminent Greek and Roman predecessors had failed with inauspicious results: the tyrant Periandros, Demetrius Polyorcetes, the king of Macedonia, Julius Caesar and Caligula. Nero made a titanic attempt to challenge the deity and legends flowered. Some said that at the first blow dealt with a pickaxe by the emperor himself blood came

gushing from the ground, together with the groans and howls of phantoms. In reality the work was held up only because of the inadequacy of the resources available and came to a standstill, as was predictable, on the death of Nero: the emperor who had also recruited gigantic legionaries and organised a dangerous to the mountains of the Caucasus populated by monstrous beings, or had tried in vain to measure with ingeniously makeshift means the deepest gulfs of Lake Alcyonius, where Dionysus had descended to Hades to restore the Moon to earth. In the wake of the myth of Ulysses the emperor appears therefore, though to an excessive degree, a man eager to probe the limits of human possibility, seeking to explore the boundaries of the world though devoting his greatest attention to the city of Rome. The villa built near Subiaco is outstanding by its originality and technical daring, laid out as a series of pavilions set at different heights by the shores of lakes and waterfalls, created by damming the upper course of the Anio and then modelled in the rugged terrain, among Nero's various urban buildings (such as the markets, the baths, the circus, etc.). At the same time one of his most famous buildings was undoubtedly the wooden amphitheatre erected in the Campus Martius, which aroused comment for the endless tiers of seats rising to the sky, an immense embroidery of stars. Even the fiercest detractors of the emperor has to acknowledge the effectiveness of his notable town-planning rules introduced after the fire of 64 AD. They regulated the materials used for the construction of buildings, their heights and the distance between them, the requirement to add internal courtyards and porticoes surmounted by terraces from which the *vigiles siphonarii*, the firemen of antiquity, could pour water on fires, and the layout of the streets, creating broad carriageways between the blocks. But it was above all the unpopular follies of the Domus Aurea, only partly completed and even that part poorly preserved, that embodied experiments in architecture and civil engineering that proved innovative at Rome. (*N.G.*)

The *stagnum Neronis*, supplied with water from the aqueduct on the Coelian hill, thus formed the focus of the architectural complex, of which the part we know best from the sources and archaeological surveys is the pavilion on the Oppian. After another destructive fire in 104 AD, Trajan built his baths over it, using Nero's structures as substructures. This circumstance saved the only building that was left of the Domus Aurea, part of which can now be visited. Excavations and research conducted in the second half of the 20th century have radically changed and extended our knowledge of Nero's residence, enabling us to guess with a fair degree of accuracy its original plan. To build this pavilion, which extended for about 370 metres from east to west, while its present length is about 240 metres, it proved necessary to alter the contours of the hills, making an artificial cut where a sill of concrete forming the foundations, almost 100 metres wide, could be embedded. On the west side a high retaining wall was raised, while on the north were two long cryptoporticuses with the double function of protecting the rooms from the damp of the ground behind and facilitating and isolating the passage of the staff. What remains is probably only the front part of the complex, whose rear extended directly to the summit of the hill, laid out in pavilions and gardens as shown by significant traces, including a *euripus* (channel) found in the eighties (the Fabbrini excavations).

But the pavilion facing the valley clearly formed a self-contained unity, with a structure in *opus testaceum*, mixed of broken brick and tiles, without

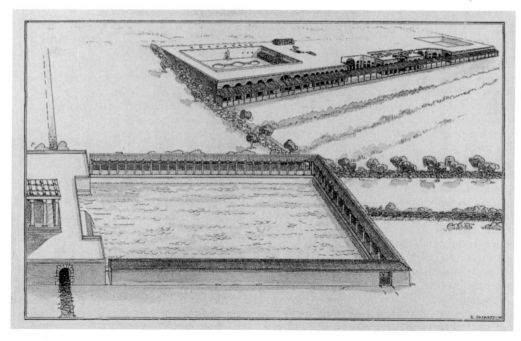

On page 244
Of the few surviving portraits of Nero, who was sentenced to *damnatio memoriae*, the Palatine portrait, which dates from 59–64 AD, is perhaps the most attractive, both by its workmanship and because it has been reliably identified: the massive head of the Domitians, the downy beard carved in the Greek marble, the rather soft fleshiness of the face and the hair combed in the Julian-Claudian fashion. Above all the skilful interplay of light and shade suggests the complex personality of the emperor before his marked psychological degeneration in the last years of his reign.

Conjectural reconstruction of the pavilion of the Oppian Hill and the *stagnum Neronis* (Elio Paparatti).

Room no. 73, imprint of a floor in *opus sectile*.

Room with the "vault of the little owls" (29) with clearly visible the imprint left by the marble facing on the cement.

courses of *bipedali*, and laid out on two storeys. The second storey was clearly flanked by the terrace and ended in the ridge, which dated from the time of Trajan, once communicating across scenic flights of steps, as was customary in the Roman architectural tradition, exemplified in large Late-Republican shrines and the villas devoted to *otium*. The plan was arranged in harmony with the cardinal points and distinguished by a marked symmetry of parts in the equivalence of the masses of masonry. The rooms were arranged around two pentagonal courtyards that linked the west and east sides. This has diminished the arguments that led to the rebuilding of two areas quite different architecturally and also chronologically: to the east the magnificent, highly original mixtilinear area with public functions and to the west the complex of apartments laid out on an orthogonal pattern of an almost traditional kind.

Here the tablinum (bed-chamber) has been fancifully identified with two pendant alcoves with their wardrobes and small rooms annexed to them, which might have accommodated the passionate nights of Nero and Poppea, lost lovers appearing on the waves where the moon shone. In reality all of these chambers, which lack doors, services and heating, must have been used for official functions or entertainments for the emperor and his guests, with the building set in a rich frame of natural beauties and works of art. The rather awkward, incoherent way the rooms interlock was probably determined by the earlier structures, like the massive load-bearing walls of the *horrea* (warehouses) or of numerous Republican houses, which were preserved without aligning them harmoniously, such was the hurry to complete this immense enterprise. From ancient authors, moreover, we know that many parts of the house were clearly never finished. Certainly the front of the palace was uni-

Fabullus in the Prison of His Art

Although it does not really mean "fabulous," the name Fabullus (recent critical interpretations of the codices actually suggest it should be Famulus or Amulius) has a symbolic value by the fascination his fanciful paintings exerted over the artists of the Renaissance. Pliny gives us a concise but shrewd description of this sublime creator. "Also the painter Famulus lived not long ago, grave and severe and at the same time florid and moist. He painted a Minerva that followed the viewer from wherever it was observed. He used to paint for very few hours a day but with great solemnity, always dressed in a toga, even when he was up on the scaffolding. The Domus Aurea was like the prison in which his art was contained; for this reason no work of his exists outside it." Pliny uses two paired terms that shows his mastery of the terminology of Greek portraiture and represents the personality and the style of this great master: according to a tradition that goes back to Fabius Pictor (4th century BC), "austere" meant that painting became a practice suitable for a noble Roman, inspired and worthy to represent mythical subjects, employing a wealth of colours (cinnabar red, deep blue, purple, indigo and green), brilliant and fluid in keeping with that wholly colouristic conception of painting by touches of colour, almost impressionistic, which became Style IV, typical of the period of Nero and Vespasian. The importance attributed to Fabullus and the architects of the palace, Severus and Celeres, reveals the momentary dominance of charismatic artists who renewed the close relationship established in the Hellenistic age with the absolute sovereign, in this case Nero, a character gifted with an outstanding aesthetic sensibility. It was Nero who commissioned the Minerva mentioned above, a goddess who had a special symbolic significance in Nero's imperial mission, which was multi-directional and powerful as the divine gaze. At the same time the idea of animation and motion in the image had close affinities with the coeval tendencies found in agile and sinewy Asiatic rhetoric or in Senecan prose. The Latin text also seems to suggest the work of a solitary painter, withdrawn into his individualism and working without assistants. It is for this reason that the painter was credited with the creation of outstanding large mythological scenes, now surely lost, of which a formal echo may be reflected only by the largest panels, like the scene of *Achilles at Skyros*, and certainly not in the decorations, which reveal a refined incomprehension of the architectural magnificence of the whole. (*N.G.*)

fied and harmonious, with a barrel-vaulted portico running its whole length. It was light that dominated the complex, penetrating the dense built fabric of the complex, with its courtyards, radial peristyles and nymphaeums, or its simple but carefully placed windows with architraves, set in walls that were like fretted screens while clearly retaining their structural validity. In the original intention, therefore, shafts of light must have pierced the interior everywhere—even through the mouths of wolves that decorated the secondary cryptoporticus—until their reflexes even reached suites of rooms laid out on carefully studied optical axes and refracted shimmering on the mosaic and marble surfaces of the most sumptuously decorated rooms. The emperor was nurtured by these reflections of Phoebus Apollo, going so far as to absorb into his palace a temple dedicated to Fortune entirely built out of a rare phosphorescent alabaster mined in Cappadocia, so that—as Pliny comments—"thanks to the stone, even when the doors were closed, inside it glowed like daylight." The ancient brightness has inexorably faded in the dark hypogeum. Adapted to these immense volumes, to judge from the traces left on the plasterwork, there must have been marble cladding. In the floors the most sumptuous *opus sectile* was preferred to mosaic; the walls were faced to a fair height, sometimes to the imposts of the vault, with orthostates in coloured marbles lined with pilaster strips and surmounted by bands and cornices.

The pictorial decoration, with its febrile handling and the immense surfaces to be covered, failed to rise to the heights of the highly imaginative building, which is truly astonishing, as can be seen on this visit, for example, in the Octagonal Room. Perhaps we have lost, however, the series of large scenes by

East wing room no. 81, holes for mounting a false ceiling with the cane chamber technique.

the mythical Fabullus, who alternated bold foreshortening with distant perspectives, and successfully coordinated the real illusion of architecture already in the Vesuvian villas. What remains after the damage inflicted by time, except for the best-known panels where we find a valuable freedom of composition, though set on an undeniably Greek iconographic matrix, is not a particularly varied series of frescoes and stuccos distinguished by an obsession with miniaturist detail, with threadlike patterns organising the spaces. The whole is dominated by decorations set against flat backdrops that generate pictorial visions expressive of *horror vacui*, where the living creatures, men or animals, have the same decorative significance as the vegetable forms or the monstrous distortions.

Just as they were, cut off, unfortunately, from any real architectural relationship with the interiors, the artists of the Renaissance saw them at first hand in all their lost brilliancy, and felt empowered to transform them into an original and inexhaustible repertory of decorative motives.

Once Upon a Time: from Rediscovery to Myth

While the three emperors of the anarchy of 69 AD intended to remain faithful to their predecessor–Vitellius himself seems to have allocated 50 million *sestertii* to completion of the work—the Flavian dynasty, which wanted to free itself in a hurry from the awkward legacy bound up with Nero's absolutist conception of power, adopted a policy of restoring these immense spaces to public use. Vespasian, for example, drained the pool with its luxuriant vegetation and built on its bed a mountain of stone, Rome's first permanent amphitheatre, where he offered the citizens lavish shows to win their favour. By an irony of fate the people called it the Coliseum because of its association with the colossal statue of Nero as *Sol Invictus*, which remained in the vicinity.

The earlier road network was restored and what were meant to be the baths of the Domus Aurea become the baths of Titus. At the same time the decline of some parts of the pavilion led to the inevitable theft of the tapestries and the reuse by small craftsmen of the far too large rooms, which were divided up vertically or horizontally to suit their special requirements. After the terrible fire of 104 AD it was Trajan, on the advice of Apollodorus of Damascus, who chose to base his baths on Nero's solid structures. A general landfill sealed the "House of Gold," already stripped of its marbles and incredible works of art, which were exhibited by the Flavians in the Forum of Peace. So these rooms, now buried underground, were used as passages and lodgings by the staff of the baths: in one of them they stored the firewood to heat the water of the *caldarium*. Only the little west rooms, which escaped being filled in, were used to house, in late antiquity, a Christian oratory dedicated to Santa Felicitas and her seven children martyred under the Antonines. But already the silence and oblivion had taken possession of one of the architectural wonders of the ancient world. Its rediscovery took place by chance around 1480 when, after a millennium, some inquiring souls with a passion for antiquity lowered themselves down ropes into the caves, through holes still visible today. They were probably searching for those

Ideal reconstruction of the
room of the Domus Aurea
with the Laocoön in the famous
painting by G. Chedanne,
19th century. Musée
des Beaux-Arts, Rouen.

marbles that were resurfacing from the rich Roman subsoil during the papacy of Sixtus IV, a patron of art and culture, to whom we owe the donation of the celebrated bronzes to the City of Rome.

*Gianni Guadalupi quotes an anonymous sonnet with
an amusing description of one of these gruelling trips into
the obscure recesses of the earth, undertaken with such
nonchalance: "We'll crawl on our bellies, with bread, ham,
apples and wine, to be more bizarre at the grottoes. And our
guide will be Master Pinzino, who gets our face and eyes all
grubby, each of us looking just like a chimney sweep,
and showing us barrels, frogs, little owls, barn owls and
night-jars, breaking our backs with our knees."*

We can imagine the amazement of the first explorers to set eyes on the *ruinate grotte*, viewed in the light of the torches populated by a pictorial fauna far more impressive than the bats troubled by the light. The discovery provoked the same stir as, two hundred years later, the frescoes of the cities buried by Vesuvius. It was the first great find of ancient painting ever to be revealed,

The Lost Gallery

Though in 1547 now fewer than twenty-five statues were exhumed, the discovery of the Domus Aurea did not, unfortunately, bring to light the great Greek masterpieces that, as the words of Pliny the Elder seem to confirm, must have been displayed in the chambers of the princely residence.
It is hardly surprising that a philhellenic spirit like Nero's should have removed many sculptural treasures from Greece to Rome: we know his collection included a very fine statue of an Amazon from Athens and a famous portrait of Alexander the Great sculpted by Lysippus, which the emperor had coated with gold, revealing a taste verging on kitsch. A recent theory suggests that the Octagonal Room contained the bronze originals of the dying Galatian and of the Galatian committing suicide, which were part of the votive offering placed on the terrace of Athena Nikephoros on the acropolis of Pergamum, until they were carried away in the brutal raid of 64 AD. In this case Nero would never have been satisfied with attractive copies like those ordered by Caesar to celebrate his conquests of the Gauls, as mentioned above.
A tradition that developed in the seventeenth century, prompted by the Homeric cycle depicted on the walls and vaults, praised highly by Nero, held that the Laocoön, "the masterpiece of the arts," was placed in the Room of Hector and Andromache, as is evocatively recorded in

a 19th-century painting. But the group was recovered on 1 June 1506 by the owner of a vineyard near the Sette Sale. It was in a room included in the area of the Domus Aurea still used by the emperor Titus and subsequently annexed to the baths of Trajan, before being buried in late antiquity with the dereliction of the whole complex. The discovery immediately responded to a deep-seated craving and exerted a considerable influence over Renaissance perceptions of antiquity. The architect Giuliano da Sangallo and Michelangelo, summoned to the site by pope Julius II, confirmed the judgment of Pliny: that group representing a priest and his sons enfolded in the coils of a serpent was wonderful and seemed "to breathe the perfume of immortality". Michelangelo did not feel capable of restoring that statue that was long considered an original rather than a fine copy in marble of a Hellenistic bronze, like those commissioned by Tiberius for his grotto at Sperlonga. Its reputation soared: Julius II purchased it and had it borne in triumphal procession to the garden of the Belvedere, one of the first nuclei of the Vatican Museums; Leo X rejected the blackmail of Francis I, king of France, who claimed it as booty of war. In 1797 the French finally succeeded in taking it off to Paris, but after the fall of Napoleon it returned to the Vatican. (*N.G.*)

enthusiastically visited by the greatest artists of the age, who ventured trembling in fear of the darkness and sudden falls but burning with excitement at the discovery. So Pinturicchio, all gold and lapis lazuli, trinkets, frills and tinsel, Perugino, Filippino Lippi, the son of a scandalous liaison between a monk and a nun, Ghirlandaio, Raphael, who left off painting to organise expeditions underground with his assistants (Giovanni da Udine, Giulio Romano, Polidoro da Caravaggio). We can still see their names carved or traced in lampblack on the walls, perhaps as signs of an objective gained in their explorations or as clues to help them find their way back through those murky labyrinths. And so antiquity was seen in colour...

These artists drew inspiration from the bizarre decorations they copied into notebooks by the light of candles. They then decorated the interiors of important Renaissance palaces and villas in the ancient style (Agosto Chigi's Farnesina, Villa Madama, even the sacred loggias and apartments of the Vatican or the Carafa chapel in the church of Santa Maria sopra Minerva in Rome), imitating with painstaking care in paint and stucco the elegant columns, candelabra and shells, the fantastic garlands and the inexhaustible proliferation of tendrils, pavilions of blades of grass, animals, pyramids suspended over a void, pierced masks and genre scenes set at carefully calculated points of the general decorative scheme, conceived as a form of visual play.

In this way they created—as Benvenuto Cellini tells us in his *Life*—the model of the "grotesque," so-called from their original location in the "grottoes" and so sarcastically described by

Vasari: "They are a kind of highly licentious and ridiculous painting, applied by the ancients to the decorations of rooms, where all that suited some places were light and airy things; so there they painted all these licentious monsters, oddities of nature and quirks and caprices of their creators, who worked in these things without any rule. They would suspend from a slender thread a weight it could never support, or give a horse legs made of leaves, a man the legs of a crane, with endless mysteries and riddles; and the artist who imagined the weirdest things was held to be the cleverest of all."

Nevertheless, a model of taste had been created. Like the wave of Egyptomania that followed Napoleon's Egyptian campaign, it was widely imitated throughout Europe: in France, under Francis I and Henri II, who invited Italian artists to cover their walls with the new decorative grammar; at the Spanish court, where the Portuguese artist Francisco de Hollanda confidently reproduced the frescoes from the Domus Aurea, as shown by his precious manuscript.

So the spread of the grotesque style was due to systematic reproductions of the decorations in the centuries that followed and encouraged the uncovering of further portions of the palace, with endless new surprises. One famous exploration of some rooms was conducted by Pier Sante Bartoli, whose drawings, reflecting Bellori's idea of the beautiful, were published in 1706. In 1774 the Roman antiquarian Mirri had sixteen more rooms cleared and commissioned the Polish painter Smugliewicz and the Italian architect Brenna to make drawings of the decorations. The result was an elegant album of sixty engravings, faithfully printed by Carloni, that was sold in various luxurious editions on the antiquarian market. It was titled *Le antiche camere delle Terme di Tito*. A particularly attractive one had plates touched up in watercolour or more boldly in tempera and is now in the Louvre.

Though a faithful survey had already been made in the 16th century of the true Baths of Titus, this was the name given to the site before the 19th centu-

ry identified it correctly. These iconographic sources are valuable today because they help us understand critically the kinds of images that prompted some inventions in the period, certainly the brilliant original colours of the paintings, the way they were skilfully framed in gilt stucco mouldings, today unfortunately dulled and fragmentary, after five hundred years of excavations, the making of copies and tracings, and heavy-handed intervention, which have compromised their clarity and even their preservation. So all honour and merit to the Italian and foreign artists, as expressed in the poem by Perin del Vaga cited by André Chastel. (*N.G.*)

> *"The poet and painter go together,*
> *And their ardour aims at a single mark,*
> *As expressed on these pages will appear,*
> *Adorned with works and worthy devices.*
> *Of this Rome gives us an example:*
> *Rome, the receptacle of all famed genius,*
> *From whose caves where none ever dwell,*
> *Now such light and such great art returns."*

Nero, an Eccentric Host

"You see, I really am an artist in all things,
I cannot live an ordinary life...
How vulgar the world will be when I'm not here any more!"
Henryk Sienkiewicz, Quo vadis?

"He resented nothing so much as being taunted that he was a poor lyre-player or being called Ahenobarbus instead of Nero." So Suetonius censured the sovereign of too many murders, of too many wives, of too many lovers, of too many pleasures, and of too great expense, by stressing his ambitions as a singer. Nero's ancestry comprised two important Roman dynasties, the Domitians and the Julian-Claudians, the *gens* founded by Caesar and given lustre by his successors. The author of the *Lives of the Twelve Caesars* gives a precise physical description. "He was of almost normal size but had a spotted and foul-smelling body, his hair was fair and its face was more attractive than graceful. He had blue eyes and a very weak, big neck, prominent belly, delicate legs and excellent health." His father, an arrogant patrician and far from irreprehensible, died only three years after Nero's birth. He failed to pass on anything but the reddish colour of his beard, hence the hateful appellation of Ahenobarbus, which Lucius Domitius certainly used in preference to Nero. Nero meant "strong" but its associations with infernal darkness led Christians

Fragments of a portrait
of Agrippina Minor from
Ostium. Museo Nazionale
Romano, Palazzo Massimo
alle Terme, Rome.
Seductive and uninhibited in his
calculating, cultivated and
fecund lust, Agrippina was
capable of ensnaring the minds
of philosophers and of
emperors.

This portrait, identified as
the young Nero, can be dated to
between 55 and 59 AD by
comparing it with coins with
the same iconography, which
is close to Augustan models,
as reflected by Nero's policies
in the early years of his reign.
Palatine Museum, Rome.

Marble head of Poppaea Sabina.
Museo Nazionale Romano,
Palazzo Massimo alle Terme,
Rome.

to create the tradition of Nero as Antichrist, the symbol of evil. A great deal depended on his very special mother, the well-known Agrippina Minor, the sister of the crazy Caligula, who made his horse a senator, but she was also the daughter of the great general Germanicus. It was she, determined with diabolical lucidity to attain her aims at all costs, who put a boy of seventeen on the throne of the world, even though a fortune-teller had foreseen that he would murder his mother. And it was not an easy enterprise... Already banished to Pontia because she was guilty of a conspiracy against her brother, she left the son born of her first marriage to the precepts of a barber and a dancer. Her second husband, the emperor Claudius, had a natural and legitimate heir, Britannicus, who then died, barely an adolescent, by the hand of Nero, who saw him as a rival. The empress had succeeded in getting Claudius to adopt her son and to make him marry the fourteen-year-old Octavia—the daughter of the emperor and of the unfortunate nymphomaniac Messalina, who had had her throat cut—after being accused unjustly of adultery, repudiated, imprisoned on the island of Ventotene and finally killed. The marriage served make the election of Nero more certain, but did not suffice. Getting rid of Claudius, who had a passion for mushrooms, involved a succulent mushroom filled with poison and the aid of the prefect of the praetorian guard Afranius Burrus. It was then 54 AD. Nero may well have cared little for power, since he was much more interested in the arts of poetry, music and painting. But to make him study the difficult art of government, his mother had entrusted him to the best tutor of the day, the philosopher Seneca. And really in the first years of his reign Nero behaved like a model pupil, acting in full respect of Republican legality. He made good laws, respected the senatorial class, ingratiated himself with the common people with generous helpings of *panem et circenses*, and in both foreign and domestic politics he showed a prudence and a moderation inspired by the example of Augustus.

But quite soon Nero showed he was no longer a puppet. He put to death Pallante, the faithful lover of his mother, and became infatuated with an Oriental freedwoman, a certain Acte. Traits gradually surfaced that scandalised the traditionalist senatorial aristocracy, which made a shudder of fear run down Agrippina's back and made her hedge her bets by favouring the young son of the deified Claudius, who, as we saw, was immediately made away with. This marked the beginning of Nero's intolerance for the precepts of his tutors, who were soon dismissed. Their divergences were political.

Nero no longer believed that the old powers (the Senate and the army) were in a position to support the Empire but that they wanted to enlarge the basis of consensus demagogically. In this he looked to Greece and the East. The cruel and grotesque aspects of the prince's behaviour concealed a tendency towards absolutism of an Oriental kind, which had been disguised but latent in the exercise of the imperial power ever since Augustus. Agrippina was no longer able to control this loose cannon, who never dreamt of winning glory at the head of the legions—though some military operations in Armenia were successful—but on the stage and in the circus, neglecting the duties of government to watch or even take part in the races.

At the same time he began to indulge his lust, his craving for wine and his greed. He also engaged in delinquent excursions in the streets of Rome dressed like a plebeian, sides of his character which no doubt helped foster the reputation of Nero in literature and later in films. In an attempt to eclipse the beauty of the conceited Poppaea Sabina, with her tawny flowing hair, with whom Nero was infatuated, it is said that Agrippina made indecent proposals to her son and even planned her murder, confirming the morbid relationship between them. To avoid incest and free himself for good from a person who had become a burden, Agrippina was accused of having made an attempt on the life of the emperor, and condemned to death, but in secret. Poisoning her would have been dangerous: anyway, knowing the risk, she had prepared herself against poison by taking antidotes. Using hired killers was equivalent to leaving his signature on the murder. Finally Nero decided to simulate an accident at sea. Invited to Baia for a festival in honour of Minerva and persuaded to embark on a ship of the kind that could be split in two by a device used in the theatres, she would perish in the waves. With the help of some fishermen she succeeded in saving herself from the wreck, but not from the sword of a centurion who caught up with her.

The sleep of the monster began to be troubled with remorse, phantoms and dark presages, in a mixture of exaltation and paranoid anguish, in a delirium of conflicting instincts. With the intention of Hellenising Roman customs, in 60 AD the emperor founded the Neronia, games to be held every five years which included contests of music, poetry, rhetoric, equitation and athletics. He himself made his debut in the guise of a charioteer and musician, four years later in Naples, the only town which, by its Greek origins, was ready to pardon his eccentricities. When Nero quavered and strummed the lyre in Rome, to the applause of his personal claque, the only way members of the audience could get out of the theatre was by pretending to be dead and having themselves carried out on a stretcher. The political situation was precipitating. Afranius Burrus died; Seneca, disgusted, withdrew to private life and devoted himself to his studies: he had hardly been a good teacher. Now short of advisors, the emperor placed the fate of the state in the hands of the prefect of the praetorian guard, the greedy and cruel Tigellinus. The fiscal pressure imposed by the splendour of the court, the trials for *lèse majesté* which aimed at the confiscation of whole estates aroused opposition even among the common people. So it happened that after the fire on 18 July of 64 AD, the rumour spread that the emperor himself had caused the disaster to make more space for the creative luxury of the Domus Aurea. In reality the fatal news of the blaze raging in Rome reached Nero in his cool seaside retreat at Antium. While, knowing the *Iliad* by heart, he could hardly have resisted reciting and even composing verses in music for new Troy as it burnt, rashly challenging Homer and Virgil in a unique literary contest, he also organised effective help for the stricken population. He threw open the monuments of the Campus Martius, turning them into makeshift shelters for the terrified survivors, and lowered the price of wheat, as well as issuing new planning regulations to avert future disaster. All the same, he had to remove the stigma of that accusation, so as a propaganda move he turned the accusation against the Christians, whom he persecuted ostentatiously. Perhaps even before Peter and Paul were martyred, their followers were burnt alive in the squares, giving the Romans a gruesome spectacle of "nocturnal illumination." The acrid stench of human flesh itself hung in the air. The enormous expenditure involved in rebuilding whole urban districts and constructing Nero's immense residence had to be paid for by an additional tribute imposed on all the provinces with exception of Greece, exempted for its cultural and athletic merits. Above all he debased the currency by reducing the amount of gold in the *aureus* and *denarius*. He had now taken the road of no return. A widespread plot supported by intellectuals and senators to kill the tyrant and hand power to the senator Calpurnius Piso was foiled by Tigellinus. A blood-letting followed. Distinguished heads rolled in the dust. Famous scholars were compelled to commit suicide: they included the poet Lucan, the writer Petronius, author of the *Satyricon* and once a refined arbiter of elegance for the emperor; Seneca himself opened his veins with Socratic resignation. Summary convictions also struck down numerous commanders stationed in the provinces, including the reliable Domitian Corbulones, who was responsible for the slight military glories of the emperor. And all this happened at the very moment when the rebellions that had broken out in Britain and Palestine were proving hard to quell. Also the emperor's family life was destroyed. After losing a daughter just four months old, his beloved Poppaea, again pregnant, suddenly died. It was rumoured that Nero himself had kicked his pregnant wife to death when she scolded him for coming home drunk. Even his affections faded: his new wife Messalina was replaced by Sporus, a castrated young man who reminded him of Poppaea, in a perverse triangle. All that remained was to fly from reality in the Greece he yearned for. An artistic tour followed, with an entourage of jugglers, artists, cooks and makeup artists stationed in Corinth, where he took part in all the Pan-Hellenic Games and, being victorious, collected more than 1,800 laurel crowns. A sad awakening followed. On his return Rome had drifted into anarchy while the legions were rebelling at the borders, acclaiming new captains who marched on Rome to overthrow the dictator. The immense rooms of the Domus Aurea were emptied. Even Tigellinus left Nero, who had his horoscope cast. The emperor was naked. As often it happens to the great, only his servants remained faithful. Fleeing from the hostile city he sought refuge in the house of the freedman Phaon and his secretary Epaphroditus. Here he received death like a coward at just thirty-one years old, uttering the famous words: "What an artist dies with me!" The words reveal a mistaken destiny. Only the compassionate Acte, who had stolen Nero's heart before Poppaea, was present to see the emperor's body laid in the earth. Inevitably the main sources paint a lurid picture of Nero's principate. The historians Tacitus, Suetonius and Cassius Dio, all directly or indirectly involved in the political opposition, delivered him to posterity as bloodthirsty and inept, one who glorified his own personality till he had himself represented as the Sun. But if we look carefully at the matter, his political and artistic ambitions must have gone far beyond everything that has been recorded of his popular image and his memory through the centuries. (*N.G.*)

The visit

Today our tour of the interior of the Domus Aurea begins from one of the brick passages in the hemicycle of the Baths of Trajan set against the front of Nero's residence. Passing through the entrance, where explanatory captions are placed on the monument, you go through one of the long barrel-vaulted galleries whose function was to support the building above. After about 40 metres, under the floor you will see the openings made in the original probes that led to the discovery of the remains of the houses obliterated when the palace was built. They had mosaic floors, with black and white tiles and **opus scutulatum** which, judging by the technique used to build the walls, might date back

On page 264
A room (no. 42) of the Domus Aurea with in the middle the marble statue of the Muse of choral poetry, Terpsichore, recovered during excavations in the post-war period. Some scholars conjecture it formed part of a group based on original by Praxiteles, which the consul Lucius Mummius brought to Rome in 146 BC after the capture of Corinth.

The entrance to the Domus Aurea in the exedra of the substructures built by Trajan.

West wing, large room in the centre of the peristyle with the "vault of the little owls."

to the 2nd century BC. From this point it is possible to get a view of a suite of rooms in the western quarter, which are still closed to the public. They were most likely built at the same time as the pavilion on the Palatine, seeing that the quarter was damaged by the fire of 64 AD. On the original façade, now screened by the portals of Trajan's building, there remain fragments of the marble base of the vaulted portico, while the interior contains, concealed from the public, the room with the "yellow vault," the room with the "black vault" and the famous room containing the "vault of the little owls" (B), where it is believed the Laocoön was placed. Its decorations were frequently copied by Renaissance painters, leading Annibale Carracci, for example, to alter his depiction of the Roman general Coriolanus.

You pass by the corner of the garden-portico (A), an attractive peristyle, no longer perceptible in its elegant breadth because it is divided by the load-bearing walls of Trajan's building, and enter the eastern area, which is laid out around two pentagonal courtyards (H). Looking up you will see you are standing under the "vault of the corridor of the eagles" (50), so called for the superb decoration, unfortunately only partly preserved: the eagles, their wings outstretched, alternate on the *clipei*, with peacocks and other birds heraldically opposed at the sides of candelabra of vegetation, caryatids and gryphons set

within red and blue fields of colour. They form a splendid frame for the central panel, a lyrical representation of Ariadne abandoned by Theseus.

The gaze is inevitably captured by the brilliancy of the crystalline marble of a statue: the draped and seated figure of Terpsichore, the muse of choral poetry, found during excavations in the post-war period. It stands out against the deep red walls (room no. 42). One of the rare sculptures preserved in these interiors, it is exceptionally significant in relation to the plan of decoration adopted by the emperor poet.

Without realising it, we have entered one of the most interesting of all the architectural achievements of the pavilion: the Nymphaeum of Ulysses and Polyphemus (C). Today we have to use our imagination to be able to fully understand the effect of perspective which must have been created by the gallery, onto which opens the large room no. 44 (now divided in two by Trajan's wall), once embellished with a double colonnade on its two short sides. From it we can distinguish the room of the nymphaeum (45), originally illuminated by the light shed from eight windows (of which two pairs out of three at the sides were subsequently converted into niches for statues), and with a waterfall which thundered down the back wall and was gathered in a pool, creating an unvarying coolness. On the vault itself is still preserved part of the mosaic set in

Room no. 42, frieze with figures in stucco on a blue ground, from which rise the columns of the architectural partitions.

a medallion—the other panels at the corners have been detached—in which we recognize without difficulty Ulysses standing and offering a cup of wine to a reclining Polyphemus. Odysseus's companions had secretly pressed grapes to make the delightful liquor, unknown to the Cyclops, whom they now intoxicated and then blinded as he slept. This episode was highly popular in nymphaea from the Julian-Claudian age for its original legendary setting: sculptural groups had already represented the episode in the cave-triclinium of Tiberius at Sperlonga, in the nymphaeum of the sunken palace of Claudius at Punta Epitaffio—a cycle that has been effectively reconstructed today in the Archaeological Museum of the Phlegreian Fields in the castle of Baia—and later decorated Hadrian's Villa at Tivoli. An effect of great realism pervades the room because of the layer of pumice covering the ceiling, a felicitous idea repeated in Renaissance and Baroque villas. Together with the frames of seashells, it helps evoke the atmosphere of a marine cavern by the precious brightness with the playful breaking of the waves in the colours of the decorations. The choice of the subject confirms the popularity surrounding the memory of Ulysses—partly because of the links with the legend of the Trojan origins of Rome—in Roman culture already in the Republican period. This is shown, for example, by the frescoes of scenes from the *Odyssey* that decorated a large residence on the Esquiline with landscapes in the mid-1st century BC. The charismatic personality of the Achaean embodied a series of qualities—not only wisdom and a thirst for knowledge but also shrewdness, courage and above all self-determination—with whom first the rich art patrons and then the powerful emperors identified themselves, qualities they would praise with their guests as they strolled at leisure admiring works of art. In other respects Nero certainly differed from the hero whom he claimed to resemble: in sense of responsibility towards others, in fidelity to his wife, in the inability to feel filial love.

We now come to the section of the east wing facing the hills. The rooms here are rather cramped because they were inserted with some difficulty against the diagonal wall of the *horrea* built by Claudius. After glancing into a

small courtyard (51), with the windows of the nymphaeum facing onto it, we go through room no. 70. This is frescoed with large architectural scenes set on different planes, with screens and coffered ceilings rendered in sharply projecting perspective, with false windows that seem to open out and frame figures, some of them disquieting, while others are simply shown offering sacrifices at aedicules. Then slender and modern figures, which might have been conceived by the genius of Le Corbusier or painted and cut out by Matisse, stand out gracefully in panels with black grounds or appear enigmatically here and there. In each room the artists have explored the range of the palette: even the highly sought-after purple-red was here used to dye the walls, so expensive because it was extracted with great labour from the murex. Our visit continues through room no. 74. This once opened on the outside, where there were the lawns of the polygonal courtyard that receded scenically towards the *stagnum Neronis* and today is covered by Trajan's landfill, while the most important state rooms were ranged on the inside.

The largest interior, laid out symmetrically, is the **"room of the gilded vault"** (D), already mentioned for its very fine decoration, whose discovery had a far-reaching influence on

Nymphaeum of Ulysses
and Polyphemus.

Nymphaeum of Ulysses
and Polyphemus, vault, detail
of the central medallion
(*emblema*) with the scene
of Ulysses offering the cup
of wine to the Cyclops.

Cryptoporticus no. 92,
architectural composition
on the wall, where set among
the panels and the usual
wreaths are fantastic animals,
birds, flowers and even some
Egyptianised figures like
the god Anubis.

decorative painting of interiors at the Renaissance. Of this wonder of the past, when the gilding and the precious marbles glittered on the walls, the marvellous stucco partitions on the barrel vault remain. The inexorable decay is captured in the splendid copies made by artists, from the watercolours of Francisco de Hollanda down to the engravings by Mirri, which show us, though not entirely faithfully, the scenes represented in the great framed panels (like the painting of Phaedra and Hyppolitus, for example, which drew on Seneca's coeval tragedy), set between fields of brilliant colour: decorations transferred to the ceilings between the 16th and 19th century. The room is surrounded by a corridor (79) which provides a significant example of Style IV decoration found in these interiors, including the less important rooms and hence much of the house: elegant candelabra and airy architectural forms open out the wall to deep perspectives set in the walls with clear panels traversed by wreaths, vine branches, slender columns on which birds perch, while there also appear small examples of landscape and interesting still lives: there is a particularly charming one of a larder with meat, a round dish, a joint and a fine cut of steaks. You turn the corner and come to a series of outer rooms which contain some true gems. We enter the long, spectacular cryptoporticus (92), which traverses the whole of the rear of the east

wing in ancient style: the light once entered it through the wolf mouths in the barrel vaulting and the window embrasures set in the walls. The fact that this was a service room is suggested by the architectural decorations, which reach down to the floor, since the walls of the most important rooms were lined in the lower register or even all the way up to the impost of the vaults with panels of coloured marble.

Bearing right, we follow one side of the pentagonal courtyard, leaving on the left the numerous rooms that interlock to form a symmetrical pattern. This brings us to the most important sector of the pavilion, which is dominated by the dimensions and original design of the octagonal room, the main attraction of the whole palace. But first it is a good idea to walk through the suite of rooms ranged along the sides. The first room (116) fortunately contains a rare example of a floor covered with a black and white mosaic which escaped Trajan's depredations because it was judged to be of minor importance. Some metres further on we find ourselves in one of the chambers that symbolise the building, the **Room of Achilles at Skyros** (E). This is a rectangular space, with walls once faced with marbles, as is shown by the imprints on the mortar. At the end of the room is a deep apse surmounted by a clamshell set in the superbly partitioned barrel vault.

Room of Achilles at Skyros, general view of the decoration of the vault and apse.

The pictorial decoration of room no. 70 with architectural scenes on two registers, with a figure at a window and slender stucco figurines.

Corridor no. 79, south wall, detail of still life with food.

In the best-preserved panel, which gives the room its name, the painting captures a famous episode of the *Iliad*: Ulysses succeeds in unmasking Achilles, hidden by his mother Thetis to keep him from war. She dressed him in women's clothing and conceals him among the daughters of Lycomedes on Skyros. Odysseus disguised himself as a merchant and brought ribbons and brooches mingled with weapons to the palace. Naturally the hero was immediately attracted to the glistening arms of a warrior. Achilles was unmasked and, wounded in his pride, he immediately brandished a spear and placed the shield on his arm, while his mother sought in vain to detain him and fear seized the unwitting maidens. If we study it carefully, the scene appears skilfully composed on different planes to simulate depth—note on the left, in the background, Ulysses, with helmet and crest, who having completed his mission is surrounded by the women, with on the right the boldly foreshortened figure of one of the princesses viewed from behind—as well as on a carefully calculated chiasmus that calms the restless symmetry of the groups in movement. A great artist must have ascended this scaffolding, light and swift in his touch, with a poetic palette that played the tones of red and blue (the favourite colours of Fabullus) set on a clear ground enlivened by stucco decorations coated with gold.

A ring of rooms, which has a decisive role in the architectural structure of the complex, surrounds and introduces us into the unreal, moving light which pervades the **Octagonal Room** (F), together with two other side-rooms set in the façade, which in ancient times faced out towards the landscape of the valley. These five rooms form a radial pattern, of which the central one (124) is another large nymphaeum with a waterfall channelled from the Caelian by an aqueduct whose arches surmount the cryptoporticus (no. 92). The two side rooms have a cruciform plan with deep niches and barrel vaulting, linked by a system of thrusts and counter-thrusts to the major barrel vault, and that in their turn to the dome of the spacious central chamber, cast in concrete. This bold piece of engineering, which had precedents in the villas or baths of Campania, and was to be repeated with greater splendour in the dome of the Pantheon and Hadrian's Villa, rests on an octagon but becomes hemispherical as it rises, without the need for spandrels, to the large central *oculus* (*lumen*), through which a soft light penetrates with an interplay of shadows, full lights and half-lights, shed by the rooms around it. These bare walls possess a simple, pure magnificence which is striking, perhaps even more so than the ancient decoration, originally rather redundant, today excessively bare. For a long time scholars naturally identified this as the room "which turned like the earth": the *coenatio rotunda*. It was, however, one of the rooms used for banquets, with the *triclinia* arranged in the spaces mentioned above as functionally communicating with each other. This arrangement may well allude to a solar symbolism, as is consistent with the hypostasis of the god Nero *Sol Invictus* and *kosmokrator*, with an allusion to the rotating vault conceived as the cosmos. Unfortunately, while the walls were predictably faced with marble, the dome supported on slender pillars—the only element that fits Suetonius's description—is completely bare and reveals no evident trace of cladding or fresco. Among the many conjectural reconstructions, there persists the theory of a false ceiling made of wood covered with thin metal sheets (pure gold?), which was made to rotate by some external mechanism activated on the surface by the hydraulic force of water, the dominant element of the Domus Aurea, or perhaps by a system of ball bearings rather like the rotating platforms for the ships at Nemi. A confirmation of the existence of an external anchorage for this rotating element was identified, many years ago, in two grooves, no longer visible, scored on the outside of the *oculus* of the dome, but L. Fabbrini thinks that at most these would have been the marks left by a covering of bronze or some other material, and thinks it is more likely that any special machinery and rooms for unusual spectacles would have been placed on the upper floor, which he rebuilt. In the absence of any hard evidence today, most scholars do not exclude the possibility that there was a machine of this kind installed to excite the admiration of guests on the Palatine, traditionally the official seat of the emperor. This might be confirmed by the discovery, among masonry dating from the Neronian period, of two circular concentric foundations that move inside a quadrangular basin. The last word, however, has yet to be said: recent careful study of the octagonal room revealed traces of iron and signs of wood in the masonry of the dome, which could have been used for coupling a tholos-

Room no. 85, trompe-l'œil window with a lakeside panorama enlivened with figures rapidly sketched in, an example of the evocative style recorded by Pliny as typical of the age of Nero. "People no longer like painted panels or surfaces which cram mountains into a bedroom: we are beginning to paint with marble. This was invented under the reign of Claudius, while under Nero they found a way to vary the uniformity by introducing touches of colour not present on the surface of the marble."

Bibliography

On the Central Archaeological Area

L. Benevolo, *Roma. Studio per la sistemazione dell'area archeologica centrale*, Rome 1985.

L. Benevolo, F. Scoppola, *L'area archeologica centrale e la città moderna*, Rome 1988.

A. Capodiferro, M.L. Conforto, C. Pavolini, M. Piranomonte, *Forma. La città antica e il suo avvenire*, Rome 1985.

Roma antiqua. "Envois" degli architetti francesi (1788–1924). L'area archeologica centrale, Rome 1985.

On the Roman Forum

A. Augenti, "Il Foro romano in età tardo-antica," in *Enciclopedia dell'arte antica classica e orientale*, Second Supplement (1971–1994), IV s.v. "Roma," Rome 1996, pp. 964–66 (with previous bibliography).

P. Carafa, "Il Foro Romano nella seconda età regia," in *Enciclopedia dell'arte antica classica e orientale*, Second Supplement (1971–1994), IV s.v. "Roma," Rome 1996, pp. 815–16 (with previous bibliography).

P. Carafa, "La valle del Foro nella prima età regia," in *Enciclopedia dell'arte antica classica e orientale*, Second Supplement (1971–1994), IV s.v. "Roma," Rome 1996, pp. 806–07 (with previous bibliography).

F. Coarelli, *Il Foro Romano, I. Periodo arcaico*, Rome 1983.

F. Coarelli, *Il Foro Romano, II. Periodo repubblicano e augusteo*, Rome 1985.

F. Coarelli, *Roma*, Laterza archaeological guide, Bari 1995².

P. Gros, M. Torelli, *Storia dell'urbanistica. Il mondo romano*, Rome-Bari 1988.

D. Palombi, "Il Foro Romano e la Via Sacra dalla media età repubblicana alla tetrarchia," in *Enciclopedia dell'arte antica classica e orientale*, Second Supplement (1971–1994), IV s.v. "Roma," Rome 1996, pp. 858–82 (with previous bibliography).

Roma, dall'antichità al medioevo, II. Contesti tardoantichi e altomedievali, edited by L. Paroli and L. Vendittelli, Milan 2004.

G. Tagliamonte, N. Purcell, C.F. Giuliani, P. Verduchi, *Forum Romanum*, in E.M. Steinby (edited by), *Lexicon Topographicum Urbis Romae*, II, Rome 1995, pp. 313–43.

P. Zanker, *Il Foro Romano. La risistemazione da Augusto alla tarda antichità*, Rome 1972.

On the Palatine and the Circus Maximus

S. Baroni, *La volta affrescata della Loggia Mattei con l'esposizione di ventidue dipinti del Metropolitan Museum of Art*, Milan 1997.

C. Cecamore, "Il Palatino dalla media età repubblicana alla tetrarchia," in *Enciclopedia dell'arte antica classica e orientale*, Second Supplement (1971–1994), IV s.v. "Roma," Rome 1996, pp. 923–30 (with previous bibliography).

P. Ciancio Rossetto, "Circus Maximus," in E.M. Steinby (edited by), *Lexicon Topographicum Urbis Romae*, I, Rome 1993, pp. 272–77 (with previous bibliography).

F. Coarelli, "La Casa di Augusto sul Palatino," in Idem, *Roma sepolta*, Rome 1984, pp. 107–45.

F. Coarelli, *Roma*, Laterza archaeological guide, Bari 1995².

P. Fortini, *Carcer Tullianum. Il Carcere Mamertino al Foro Romano*, Milan 1998.

Gli Orti Farnesiani sul Palatino, conference proceedings (Rome, 28–30 November 1985), edited by V. Cazzato, Rome 1990.

I. Iacopi, *La decorazione pittorica dell'Aula Isiaca*, Milan 1997.

G. Morganti, *Gli Orti Farnesiani*, Milan 1999.

Roma, dall'antichità al medioevo, II. Contesti tardoantichi e altomedievali, edited by L. Paroli and L. Vendittelli, Milan 2004.

Roma. Romolo, Remo e la fondazione della città, exhibition catalogue (Rome 2000), edited by A. Carandini and R. Cappelli, Milan 2000.

G. Tagliamonte, E. Papi, A. Augenti, "Palatium, Palatinus Mons," in E.M. Steinby (edited by), *Lexicon Topographicum Urbis Romae*, IV, Rome 1999, pp. 14–40.

N. Terrenato, "Il Palatino e il Germalo in età regia," in *Enciclopedia dell'arte antica classica e orientale*, Second Supplement (1971–1994), IV s.v. "Roma," Rome 1996, pp. 809–10, 818–19 (with previous bibliography).

M.A. Tomei, *Il Palatino*, Rome 1992.

M.A. Tomei, *Museo Palatino*, Milan 1997.

P. Zanker, *Augusto e il potere delle immagini*, Turin 1989 (original edition Munich 1987).

On the Capitol and the Capitoline Museums
M. Albertoni, *Archeologia in Campidoglio*, Rome 1997 (with previous bibliography).

A. Augenti, "Il Campidoglio in età tardo-antica," in *Enciclopedia dell'arte antica classica e orientale*, Second Supplement (1971–1994), IV s.v. "Roma," Rome 1996, p. 962 (with previous bibliography).

P. Carafa, "Il Campidoglio nella seconda età regia," in *Enciclopedia dell'arte antica classica e orientale*, Second Supplement (1971–1994), IV s.v. "Roma," Rome 1996, pp. 813–14 (with previous bibliography).

La Lupa Capitolina, exhibition catalogue (Rome 2000), edited by C. Parisi Presicce, Milan 2000.

Musei Capitolini, Milan 2000 (with previous bibliography).

D. Palombi, "Il Campidoglio dalla media età repubblicana alla tetrarchia," in *Enciclopedia dell'arte antica classica e orientale*, Second Supplement (1971–1994), IV s.v. "Roma," Rome 1996, pp. 845–55 (with previous bibliography).

Sculture di Roma antica. Collezioni dei Musei Capitolini alla Centrale Montemartini, edited by M. Bertoletti, M. Cima, E. Talamo, Milan 19992.

On the Imperial Forums
J.C. Anderson, *The Historical Topography of the Imperial Fora (Latomus Coll., 182)*, Brussels 1984.

A. Augenti, "I Fori imperiali in età tardo-antica," in *Enciclopedia dell'arte antica classica e orientale*, Second Supplement (1971-1994), IV s.v. "Roma," Rome 1996, pp. 966–67 (with previous bibliography).

S. Baiani, M. Ghilardi, *Crypta Balbi - Fori Imperiali. Archeologia urbana a Roma e interventi di restauro nell'anno del Grande Giubileo*, Rome 2000.

R. Bianchi Bandinelli, *Il Maestro delle imprese di Traiano*, Milan 2003[4].

C. Cecamore, *Fori Imperiali*, in *Enciclopedia dell'arte antica classica e orientale*, Second Supplement (1971–1994), IV s.v. "Roma," Rome 1996, pp. 883–91 (with previous bibliography).

C. Conti, "Gli scultori della Colonna Traiana," in *Tra Damasco e Roma. L'architettura di Apollodoro nella cultura classica*, exhibition catalogue (Damascus 2001–02), edited by F.F. Farina, G. Calcani, C. Meucci, M.L. Conforto and A.N. Al Azm, Rome 2001, pp. 199–213.

Curia, *Forum Iulium, Forum Transitorium*, edited by C. Morselli, E. Tortorici, Rome 1989.

E. D'Ambra, *Private Lives, Imperial Virtues. The Frieze of the Forum Transitorium in Rome*, Princeton 1993.

J. Ganzert, *Im Allerhiligsten des Augustusforums*, Mainz am Rhein 2000.

P. Gros, "La 'militarisation' de l'urbanisme trajanien à la lumière des recherches récentes sur le Forum Traiani," in *Traiano emperador de Roma*, conference proceedings (Seville, 14–17 September 1998), edited by J. González, Rome 2001, pp. 227–49.

I luoghi del consenso imperiale. Il Foro di Augusto. Il Foro di Traiano. Introduzione storico topografica, exhibition catalogue (Rome 1995–96), edited by E. La Rocca, R. Meneghini and L. Ungaro, Rome 1995.

I marmi colorati della Roma imperiale, exhibition catalogue (Rome 2002–03), edited by M. Di Nuccio and L. Ungaro, Venice 2002.

La Colonna Traiana, edited by F. Coarelli, Rome 1999.

E. La Rocca, *I Fori imperiali*, Rome 1995.

E. La Rocca, "Il Foro di Traiano in base alle più recenti ricerche," in *Traiano emperador de Roma*, conference proceedings (Seville, 14–17 September 1998), edited by J. González, Rome 2001, pp. 251–85.

E. La Rocca, "La nuova immagine dei Fori Imperiali," in *RM*, 108, 2001, pp. 171–213.

R. Meneghini, "Il Foro di Traiano. Ricostruzione architettonica e analisi strutturale," in *RM*, 108, 2001, pp. 245–63.

R. Meneghini, "Mercati di Traiano," in *Enciclopedia dell'arte antica classica e orientale*, Second Supplement (1971–94), IV s.v. "Roma," Rome 1996, pp. 891–93 (with previous bibliography).

J. Packer, "Templum Divi Traiani Parthici et Plotinae: a debate with R. Meneghini," in *JRA*, 16, 2003, pp. 109–36.

J. Packer, *The Forum of Trajan in Rome. A Study of the Monuments*, Berkeley 1997.

S. Rizzo, "Il progetto Fori Imperiali," in S. Baiani, M. Ghilardi (edited by), *Crypta Balbi - Fori Imperiali. Archeologia urbana a Roma e interventi di restauro nell'anno del Grande Giubileo*, Rome 2000, pp. 62–78.

S. Rizzo, "Indagini nei fori Imperiali. Oroidrografia, foro di Cesare, foro di Augusto, templum Pacis," in *RM*, 108, 2001, pp. 215–44.

Roma, dall'antichità al medioevo. Archeologia e storia, Milan 2001.

S. Settis, A. La Regina, G. Agosti, V. Farinella, *La Colonna Traiana*, Turin 1988.

M. Spannagel, *Exemplaria principis. Untersuchungen zu Entstehung und Ausstattung des Augustusforum* (Archäologie und Geschichte, 9), Heidelberg 1999.

Tra Damasco e Roma. L'architettura di Apollodoro nella cultura classica, exhibition catalogue (Damascus 2001–02), edited by F.F. Farina, G. Calcani, C. Meucci, M.L. Conforto and A.N. Al Azm, Rome 2001.

R. Westall, "The Forum Iulium as representation of Imperator Caesar," in *RM*, 103, 1996, pp. 83–118.

H. Wiegartz, "Simulacra Gentium auf dem Forum Transitorium," in *Boreas*, 19, 1996, pp. 171–79.

On the Valley of the Colosseum
Arco di Costantino. Tra archeologia e archeometria, edited by P. Pensabene, C. Panella, Rome 1999.

A. Augenti, "Il Colle Oppio e la valle del Colosseo in età tardoantica," in *Enciclopedia dell'arte antica classica e orientale, Second Supplement (1971–1994)*, IV s.v. "Roma," Rome 1996, pp. 972–73 (with previous bibliography).

A.M. Colini, L. Cozza, *Ludus Magnus*, Rome 1962.

M.L. Conforto, A. Melucco Vaccaro, P. Cicerchia, G. Calcani, A.M. Ferroni, *Adriano e Costantino. Le due fasi dell'arco nella valle del Colosseo*, Milan 2001.

A. Giuliano, *Arco di Costantino*, Milan 1955.

Il Colosseo, edited by A. Gabucci, Milan 1999.

Meta Sudans, I. *Un'area sacra in Palatio e la valle del Colosseo prima e dopo Nerone*, edited by C. Panella, Rome 1996.

R. Rea, *Anfiteatro Flavio*, Rome 1996.

Rota Colisei. La Valle del Colosseo attraverso i secoli, edited by R. Rea, Milan 2002.

Sangue e Arena, exhibition catalogue (Rome 2001), edited by A. La Regina, Milan 2001.

R. Santangeli Valenzani, "L'Oppio e la valle del Colosseo dalla media età repubblicana alla tetrarchia," in *Enciclopedia dell'arte antica classica e orientale*, Second Supplement (1971–1994), IV s.v. "Roma," Rome 1996, pp. 937–42 (with previous bibliography).

N. Terrenato, "Valle del Colosseo e Celio in età regia," in *Enciclopedia dell'arte antica classica e orientale*, Second Supplement (1971–1994), IV s.v. "Roma," Rome 1996, pp. 810, 820–21 (with previous bibliography).

On the Domus Aurea
L. Fabbrini, *Domus Aurea: il palazzo sull'Esquilino*, in E.M. Steinby (edited by), *Lexicon Topographicum Urbis Romae*, II, Rome 1995, pp. 56–63 (with previous bibliography).

I. Iacopi, *Domus Aurea*, Milan 1999.

E.M. Moormann, "'Vivere come un uomo': l'uso dello spazio nella Domus Aurea," in *Horti Romani*, proceedings from the international conference (Rome, 4–6 May 1995), edited by M. Cima, E. La Rocca, Rome 1998, pp. 345–61.

"Nerone. La vita, le follie. Le meraviglie della Domus Aurea," in *Le grandi storie di Meridiani*, edited by M. Jevolella, 1, Milan 1999.

M.-N. Pinot de Villechenon, *Domus Aurea. La decorazione pittorica del palazzo neroniano nell'album delle "Terme di Tito" conservato al Louvre*, with a historical introduction by G. Guadalupi, Milan 1998.

M. Ranieri Panetta, *Nerone. Il Principe Rosso*, Milan 1999.

E. Segala, I. Sciortino, *Domus Aurea*, Milan 1999.

For magazine articles abbreviations from the Archäologische Bibliographie (1993) have been used.

Photograph Credits

Archivio grafico, fotografico
e storico della Soprintendenza
archeologica di Roma
(Photos by Paolo Callipari,
Giorgio Cargnel, Luigi
Colasanti, Romano D'Agostini,
Gianfranco Gentile, Alessio
Giorgetti, Andrea Jemolo,
Luciano Mandato, Marcello
Martini, Eugenio Monti, Lino
Mozzano, Maurizio Necci,
Rossella Rea, Pasquale Rizzi)

Archivio grafico e fotografico
della Sovraintendenza ai Beni
Culturali del Comune di Roma
(Photos by Stefano Castellani,
Roberto Lucignani, Marina
Milella)

Archivio grafico e fotografico
dei Musei Capitolini, Rome
(Photos by Zeno Colantoni,
Araldo De Luca, Lorenzo
De Masi, Antonio Idini,
Roberto Lucignani)

Istituto Centrale per il Catalogo
e la Documentazione, Rome
(Photos by Eugenio Volpi
e Antonio Di Carlo)

Archivio Fotografico Comunale,
Museo di Roma, Rome

Archivio dell'Accademia
Americana, Roma

Archivio Scala, Antella (Florence)

Studio Inklink, Florence

Donatella Donati, Fermo

Nunzio Giustozzi, Monte Urano

Archivio Mondadori Electa /
Marco Covi

Maurizio Di Ianni, Rome

Chromamedia
(Ph. A. Panegrossi, P. Cipollina)

*We wish to express our
gratitude to Bruno Angeli,
Angela Carbonaro, Roberto
Lucignani, Luciano Mandato
and Marina Milella, who with
their specialised knowledge and
assistance kindly helped us
in the research for iconographic
material.*

*Holders of any unidentified
photograph sources should
contact the copyright holder.*

This volume was printed
by Mondadori Electa S.p.A.,
at Elcograf S.p.A.,
via Mondadori 15, Verona, in 2017